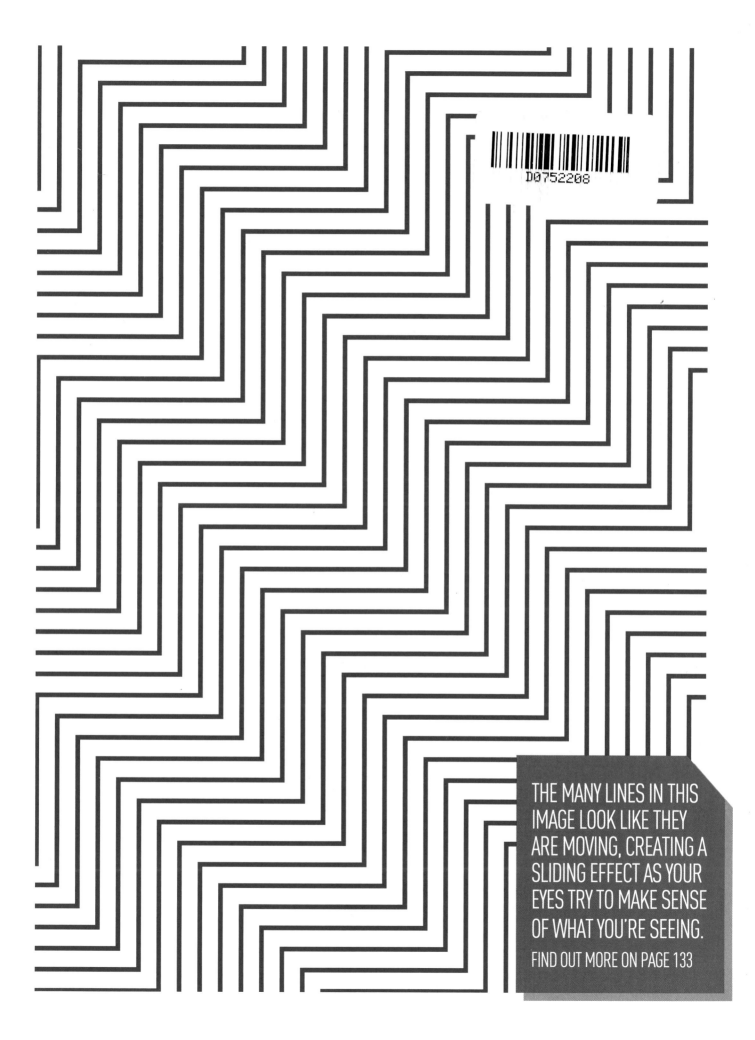

THE MANY LINES IN THIS IMAGE LOOK LIKE THEY ARE MOVING, CREATING A SLIDING EFFECT AS YOUR EYES TRY TO MAKE SENSE OF WHAT YOU'RE SEEING.

FIND OUT MORE ON PAGE 133

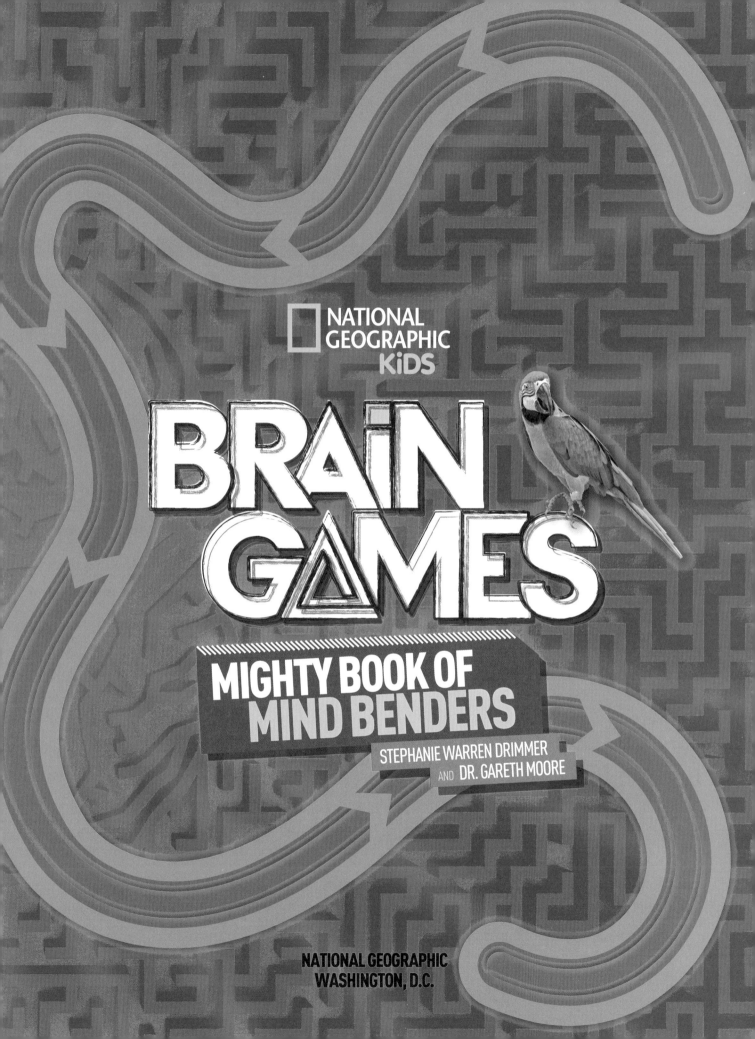

NATIONAL
GEOGRAPHIC
KiDS

BRAIN GAMES

MIGHTY BOOK OF MIND BENDERS

STEPHANIE WARREN DRIMMER
AND DR. GARETH MOORE

NATIONAL GEOGRAPHIC
WASHINGTON, D.C.

CONTENTS

CHAPTER ONE

BRAINIACS WANTED

YOUR BRAIN WEIGHS ROUGHLY THREE POUNDS (1.4 KG)— ABOUT AS MUCH AS A BAG OF SUGAR.

It looks like a pinkish cauliflower. And if you poked it, it would feel spongy and slimy.

That lump of tissue is responsible for all your thoughts and actions, your dreams, your plans, and your memories. It's what makes you you. That takes a lot of mental might. But your brain does it all on just 20 percent of the energy you take in through food. That's about the equivalent of two apples per day devoted to brain power!

Even running on that small amount of power, your brain is smarter than the most powerful supercomputer ever designed. But it uses far less energy than a computer, and it never shuts down. And, unlike your average laptop or tablet, your brain can learn new things.

The human brain is made of special cells called neurons. These cells "talk" to each other using chemical signals that hop from one neuron to another. When you learn something new, your neurons change. The connections between them become stronger, and they form new pathways to other neurons. Over time, learning can actually change the structure of your brain.

So, are you ready to see what your own brain can do? In these pages, you'll find all kinds of puzzles, games, and activities to nurture your noggin. Some of them might be a snap, while others might take multiple tries or require asking a friend for help. Along the way, you'll also learn about the most fascinating experiments and newest discoveries in brain science.

ARE YOU UP FOR A CRANIAL CHALLENGE? GAME ON! →

DIGGING INTO THE MIND

OUR FIRST ATTEMPTS TO PEER INSIDE THE HUMAN BRAIN WERE ... PRETTY GRUESOME.

LIKE A HOLE IN THE HEAD

In 2016, archaeologists working near the Nile river in the East African country of Sudan uncovered something incredible: the remains of a 7,000-year-old person. The Paleolithic-era man was curled up in the fetal position, with his knees pulled up toward his chin. He was covered with red ocher, a type of dye. A clamshell rested on his forehead. And in his skull was a hole, with smooth edges that suggested someone had drilled it on purpose. But why?

For thousands of years, our ancient ancestors practiced trepanation: the act of cutting a hole in someone's skull. Experts believe trepanation was sometimes performed for medical reasons, such as treating pain caused by brain injury or disease. Other times, the practice may have been part of a ritual believed to allow spirits to pass in or out of the body. Thousands of punctured skulls have been unearthed all over the world.

No matter why it was done, trepanation was potentially fatal and probably incredibly painful! (Ancient people hadn't yet invented anesthesia or painkillers.) Yet, this early brain surgery was likely the first time people peered inside the skull and took a peek at the brain inside.

BUMPS AHEAD

Fast-forward to the mid-19th century. People had mostly stopped drilling holes in each other's skulls in favor of a new practice: measuring them.

THERE ARE NO PAIN SENSORS IN YOUR BRAIN, BUT THERE ARE IN YOUR SKULL.

OUCH!

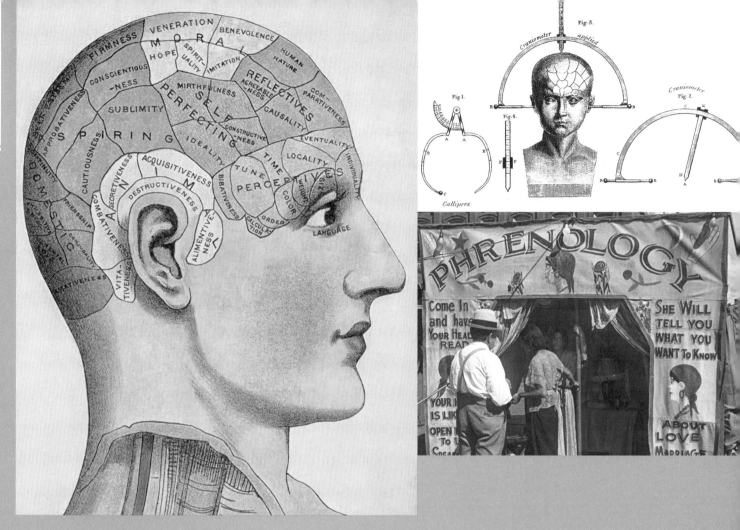

Around that time, people started to get the idea that the brain was where thoughts came from. A German doctor named Franz Joseph Gall reasoned that brain parts must be like muscles: If you exercised them, they'd grow bigger. Therefore, he thought, it was possible to study the shape of someone's skull to see what the brain within was like. Bumps on the skull would show that the brain tissue underneath was particularly strong and bulky; dents would show where it was weak.

People in the Victorian era loved the idea. Some called themselves "phrenologists" and set up shop doing head readings, charging a few pennies apiece. Using their hands, a tape measure, and a device called a craniometer, they would measure the shapes of skulls and their lumps and bumps. A round head meant you were strong and confident, whereas a square one meant you were solid and reliable. A small bump in the right place might mean you enjoyed fine dining—but if it was too big,

you were a glutton. The practice was so well accepted that employers would often send people seeking jobs to the local phrenologist to make sure they were trustworthy and hardworking.

Eventually, modern science showed that phrenology was nonsense. The bumps on your head don't say anything about your smarts or personality. But out of phrenology came one big idea: There are different areas of the brain responsible for different tasks. A new generation of brain scientists set out to create an accurate map of the mind.

THE **TERMS** "HIGHBROW," "LOWBROW," "WELL-ROUNDED," AND "GETTING YOUR HEAD EXAMINED" COME FROM **PHRENOLOGY.**

→ MAPPING THE MIND

GERMAN DOCTOR EDUARD HITZIG SAW THE BRAIN UP CLOSE AND PERSONAL.

Soldiers at Hitzig's 1870s military hospital in Nancy, France, during the Franco-Prussian War would come in with pieces of their skulls blown away. Not one to pass up an opportunity to learn something, Hitzig tried stimulating the exposed brain directly, using wires connected to a battery. He noticed something strange: When he shocked an area at the back of the brain, it made the patient's eyes move.

Over time, scientists built on Hitzig's discoveries to build the first brain maps. Today, we know that the brain is divided into different areas, called lobes. Your occipital lobe helps you process what you see, and your temporal lobe controls your hearing. Your parietal lobe helps process touch and integrates the sensory input you receive. And your frontal lobe is in charge of complex thoughts, emotions, and problem-solving.

Today, brain maps can be very detailed. Over the past few years, scientists at the Human Brain Project based in Geneva, Switzerland, have embarked on a mission to build a complete, virtual model of a human brain. It's a big job: They have to map the activity of the brain's 86 billion neurons! Someday, the researchers hope their cranium-in-a-computer will help them investigate brain diseases and also study how to build powerful brain-inspired computers.

UPLOADING THE BRAIN

Some scientists want to take things a step further. Once we've mapped every neuron in the human mind and figured out how they all communicate, we may be able to create mind maps that show how individual brains work, too. Some experts think that if we could map someone's brain activity, then turn that activity into computer code, it's possible that we could upload that code into a computer. That way, a person could live forever inside a machine.

Many other experts don't think this is possible. They don't think you can capture a person's thoughts, feelings, and memories in computer code. But much of how the brain works is still a big mystery. What will we find when we finally unravel it?

SOME **EXPERTS** HAVE PREDICTED THAT **COMPUTERS** WILL BE **SMARTER** THAN HUMANS BY 2029.

EACH **ONE** OF THE **BRAIN'S** 86 **MILLION NEURONS** IS CONNECTED TO UP TO **10,000 OTHERS.**

FRONTAL LOBE

PARIETAL LOBE

OCCIPITAL LOBE

TEMPORAL LOBE

SCI-FI SURGERY

During a July 2016 surgery to remove a tumor from the brain of a musician named Dan Fabbio, surgeons handed the patient a saxophone. Lying there on the table, awake with his brain exposed, Fabbio took a deep breath and played a song.

Why the strange surgery? During this type of operation, patients are often kept awake—their skulls are numbed so they feel no pain. Doctors do this because no two brains are exactly the same. One person's hearing center, for example, might be in a slightly different spot than another person's. So when doctors perform brain surgery to remove tumors, they want to make sure not to take out a part of the brain that will prevent someone from being able to talk, play tennis—or play the saxophone, as Fabbio does. By performing surgery while the patient is awake, doctors can keep track of which part of the brain does what task.

CHAPTER TWO

THE SENSES

The next time you go for a walk, focus on what your senses are telling you about your environment. Do you hear the crunch of leaves underfoot? Smell asphalt and dirt? Feel the air against your skin? Notice the details in the sky, plants, and buildings around you?

The senses are our brain's way of communicating with the outside world. We think of ourselves as having five of them: vision, hearing, touch, smell, and taste. But we also have many other senses, including our sense of temperature, the sense of pain, and the ability to sense the pull of gravity.

→

THE STROOP **TEST**

READ THE FOLLOWING LIST OF COLORS OUT LOUD:

ORANGE   BLUE   RED
GREEN   BLACK   YELLOW
GRAY   ORANGE   GREEN
RED   PURPLE   BLUE

This probably wasn't too hard, right? Now do it again for the words below. Say out loud the color of each word, ignoring the actual letters of the word. So for example, the word BLUE with red letters should be read out as "red." Do this as fast as you can!

ORANGE   BLUE   RED
GREEN   BLACK   YELLOW
GRAY   ORANGE   GREEN
RED   PURPLE   BLUE

[BEHIND THE BRAIN]

Did you find you were much slower the second time? If so, that's a result of something called the Stroop effect. While you're reading the second set of colors, your brain struggles between the two different interpretations of each word—one based on its actual color, and the other based on the color that the word describes. This results in a conflict that requires you to consciously think about what you're seeing, rather than letting your brain handle it automatically for you. This makes you much slower on the second set, and you might even have gotten some of them wrong without realizing it.

MAKING SENSE OF SENSES

IT MIGHT SEEM LIKE YOUR FIVE SENSES OPERATE INDEPENDENTLY. HEARING IS FOR SOUNDS, VISION FOR SIGHT, SMELL FOR ODORS. BUT THE TRUTH IS THAT OUR SENSES WORK TOGETHER TO HELP US UNDERSTAND THE WORLD.

Most of the time, this sensory collaboration happens without our even realizing it. But we can observe it working in unusual situations. For example, experiments show that silent videos of people talking activate the part of the brain that processes sound. And dyeing food strange colors changes how we perceive its taste.

SUPER SENSES

When one sense is lost, others can perform roles we didn't know they were capable of.

It might seem like we use only visual cues to orient ourselves and figure out where we are in the world. But a group of visually impaired baseball players shows that's not exactly true.

Since 1975, players in the National Beep Baseball Association in Minnesota have been hitting, catching, and running the bases—with a few tweaks. Instead of using visual cues, these visually impaired players use sound: By listening carefully to beeps coming from an oversize (one-pound [.45-kg]) softball, they can play America's pastime without ever seeing the ball.

Some blind people have even taught themselves to use this sensory ability to navigate the larger world. Like certain animals, including bats and dolphins, they get around via echolocation—the use of sound waves to determine the location of surrounding objects. They learn to make sounds and clicks, then listen back for how the sound waves bounce off nearby objects. These sound waves identify where the objects are and even how big they are.

BEEP BASEBALL PLAYER, 1993

WoW!

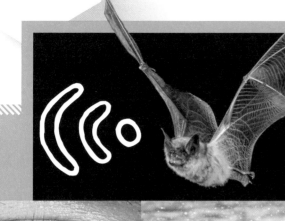

MIXED-UP SENSES

For some people, the way the senses work together is extremely powerful. People with a brain condition called synesthesia make sense of sensory information using multiple senses at once. For example, viewing a sunset might make someone with synesthesia taste blackberries. The sight of moving dots might sound like violins, or the written word "school" might appear surrounded in a halo of green. For synesthetes, the world is a constant jumble of sensation.

Scientists used to think synesthesia was very rare. But now, they think there are probably many people who have this condition and don't even know it. One young woman only learned she was a synesthete after she attended a college lecture about the condition. Experts think as many as 1 in 200 people might see, hear, or taste the world this way.

SYNESTHESIA IS HEREDITARY: **40 PERCENT** OF SYNESTHETES SAY THEY HAVE A CLOSE RELATIVE WITH THE CONDITION.

MAGIC SHAPES

TAKE A LOOK AT THESE THREE PICTURES. IN EACH CASE, DO YOU SEE A SHAPE IN THE MIDDLE?

[BEHIND THE BRAIN]

The pictures simply show some circles with gaps in them. However, your brain is so good at breaking the visual world down into shapes and objects that it assumes the shapes must actually be there. That's because the partial circles make less sense to it than the alternative. This works even when you're imagining a complex shape, like the five-pointed star above.

MAGIC COLOR

CAN YOU SEE A PINK SQUARE IN THE CENTER OF THIS ILLUSTRATION? Is the paper also slightly pink?

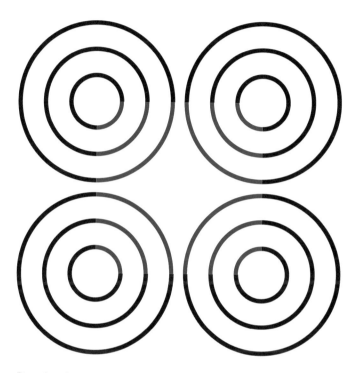

Your brain can even repair objects so they appear the way it thinks they should. You can test this out with this tennis-ball-like picture below. For it to work, you need to stare at the orange dot without moving your eyes away for 15 seconds or so. As you stare at the orange dot, do the white lines disappear, magically merging the separate segment back into the full circle?

Despite the appearance of a pink square, the paper is exactly the same shade of white all over. Your brain is showing you the pink square as its explanation for the partially pink circles. It is assuming that there is something pink obscuring parts of the circles, and from the position of the pink areas, it assumes that the shape is a square.

ARROW ASSESSMENT

LOOK AT THE TWO HORIZONTAL LINES between the heads on each pair of arrows. Which line do you think is longer—the top one or the bottom one?

Surprisingly, both lines are exactly the same length. Check using a ruler if you'd like! Your brain is influenced by the shape of the heads, which make you feel that the bottom line is probably longer. This is because the angled parts of the arrowheads take up more space to the left and right—and your brain thinks this even though you know they aren't actually part of the horizontal line at all.

SPACED OUT

DO THE GAPS BETWEEN THESE RECTANGLES GET BIGGER AS YOU LOOK LEFT TO RIGHT ALONG THE ROW?

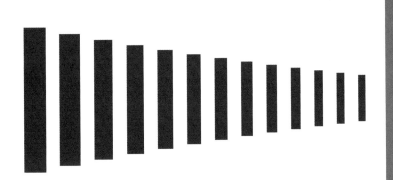

Amazingly, the gap between every pair of neighboring rectangles is exactly the same!

[BEHIND THE BRAIN]

So why do they look like they get farther apart? It's all due to the way they're arranged, which your brain interprets as if they are a set of posts vanishing into the distance. If that were true, then as they got smaller with distance the appearance of the gap between them would also get smaller with distance. When this doesn't happen, as it didn't here, your brain "knows" that they must be getting farther apart. In reality, this is a really useful calculation for your brain to make automatically for you. It only goes wrong when looking at pictures like the above, which have been deliberately drawn to trick you!

RAIL TRACK ILLUSION

TAKE A LOOK AT THESE RAILWAY TRACKS and the red rectangles that have been drawn on top. Which of the two red rectangles is larger?

In fact, both red rectangles are identical—exactly the same width and height, with exactly the same shadow beneath them.

[BEHIND THE BRAIN]

The reason the upper rectangle looks larger is because your brain is interpreting the entire image as a 3D scene, even though it knows that there wouldn't actually be red rectangles floating over any real railway tracks.

In a 3D scene, things look smaller as they get farther away, and so your brain assumes that the upper rectangle must "in real life" be larger, since the rails that it is comparing its size against have gotten smaller with distance.

FLICKERING DOTS

MOVE YOUR EYES AROUND THIS PURPLE GRID, looking at the various orange dots. What do you see?

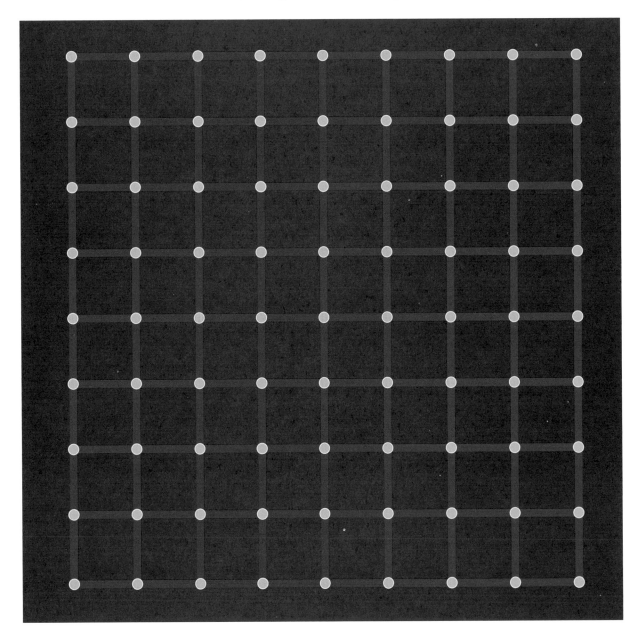

As you look around the grid, the orange dots that you aren't directly looking at appear to become suddenly hollow, showing through to the black background behind. The reason for this effect is not yet understood, but it is a good demonstration of just how much automatic processing of your vision goes on in your brain without your conscious control!

BUBBLE TRAILS

IMAGINE

FOCUS ON ONE OF THESE YELLOW BUBBLES FOR A BRIEF MOMENT, then move your eyes to another bubble, and then to another, and so on. What do you see?

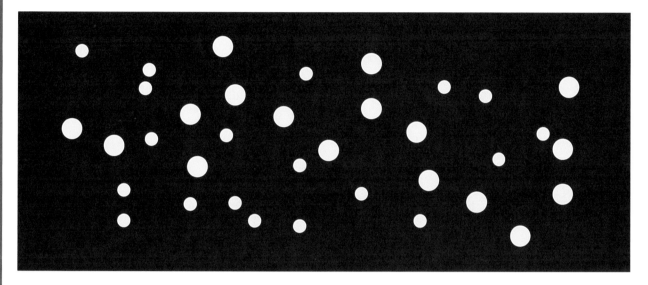

As you move your eyes around the image, do you see extra dark blue bubbles appear and then fade away?

FRENZIED FLOWERS

THESE 16 SETS OF LINES, EACH ARRANGED IN A CIRCLE, look a little like a field of flowers when viewed from above. As you look at them, what do you see?

Do you see a shimmering effect as you look at each flower? The lines that make up each flower have only small gaps between them as they near the center, which—combined with the strongly contrasting background—makes it confusing for your eyes. The result is that they seem to shine or shimmer in their centers.

THE PURPLE VASE

WHAT DO YOU SEE HERE? IT IS INDEED A PURPLE VASE, but there's more to it than that. Can you see why?

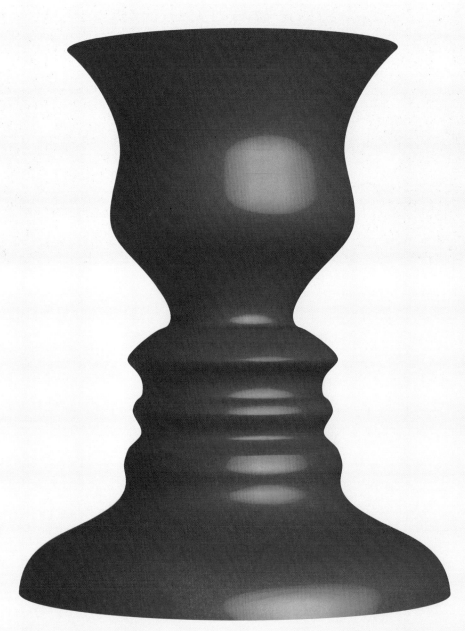

If you look at the areas to the left and right of the vase, do you see two faces looking at each other? You see the faces because the vertical profile of each side of the vase is in the shape of a side-on view of a face. Your brain is so good at spotting faces that it is able to see them even in the outline of a simple vase!

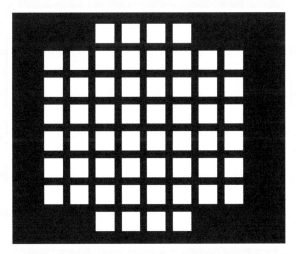

FLOATING BALL

TAKE A LOOK AT THESE TWO BALLS:

Does the ball on the right look like it is floating slightly above the page?

[BEHIND THE BRAIN]

The ball on the right looks like it is floating because of the shadow behind it, which, when compared with the shadow behind the ball on the left, is much farther away from the ball. Your brain interprets the distance of the shadow from the ball as indicating that the ball on the right must be in the air, which can make it appear to float slightly above the page.

FLOATING SURFACE

THIS SIMPLE ARRANGEMENT OF SQUARES HIDES AN INTERESTING EFFECT. As you look around it, what do you see?

Did you see pale circles appearing in the gaps between the squares? This is once again a product of your brain's visual system that no one is yet able to fully explain!

SHIMMERING DIAMONDS

RUN YOUR EYES AROUND THIS IMAGE IN CIRCLES AS WELL AS IN STRAIGHT LINES. Do these diamond rings appear to shimmer?

[BEHIND THE BRAIN]

Although the effect is less powerful than with narrow lines, the small and heavily contrasting shapes in this image can trick your brain into thinking that the image is shimmering. It happens here too because of the strong contrast and the narrow gaps, accompanied by the lack of an obvious place to focus your attention.

DOING THE WAVE

LOOK AT THIS PICTURE, SLOWLY MOVING YOUR EYES AROUND IT. What do you see?

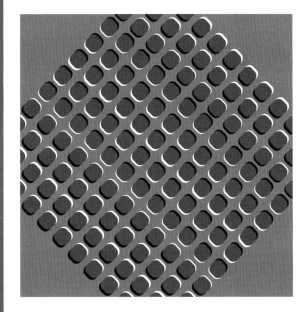

Does it look like the diagonal columns of shapes are gently swaying back and forth?

[BEHIND THE BRAIN]

The reason for this wavelike movement effect is the white and black edges on the sides of the blue shapes that vary from column to column. Your eye interprets them as light and shadow, but because they change from column to column, your brain is continually reinterpreting what it thinks is your viewpoint as it looks at different shapes. The result of this is a strange swaying motion as your brain mentally moves the shapes to where it now thinks they must actually be placed.

YELLOW ALERT!

LOOK AT THIS SHIMMERING PICTURE ... but not for too long, since it can make your eyes start to hurt!

[BEHIND THE BRAIN]

The crazy shimmering effect appears whenever you move your eyes around this image, as long as you don't have the book too far away from you. It happens because your eye doesn't have any strong features to latch on to. With such heavily contrasting, narrow lines, the parts of your eye that are exposed to bright and dark areas are continually changing, creating very strong changes in light on the retina at the back of your eye. Without any features to anchor your perception of the image, your brain struggles to make sense of the scene and you see a flickering, shimmering picture.

THREE IN ONE

IF YOU MIX DIFFERENT COLORS OF PAINT, YOU END UP WITH NEW COLORS THAT DON'T MATCH ANY OF THE COLORS YOU STARTED WITH. A similar effect can happen even when you don't mix the colors! Take a look at this picture. Do you see three shades of green, three shades of pink, three shades of orange, and three shades of blue?

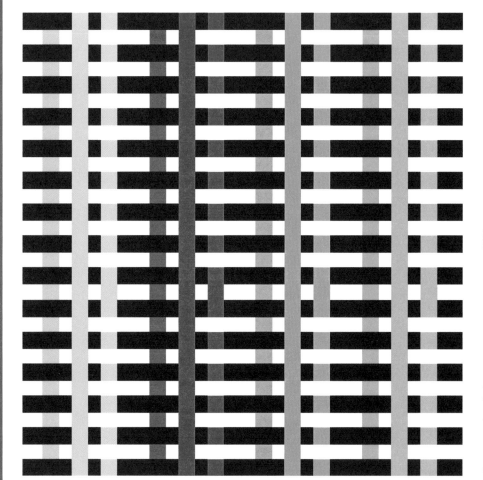

Amazingly, there is in fact only one shade of green, one shade of pink, one shade of orange, and one shade of blue!

[BEHIND THE BRAIN]

The overlapping black and white bars are altering how you see each of the colors. The way your brain interprets a color is heavily influenced by the other colors nearby, because your brain treats any picture as if it were a real-life scene. The assumption is that the area where the bright, white bars are crossing must be brightly lit, and so the color appears brighter. Your brain thinks it must be less well lit where the dark, black bars are crossing, and so the color appears dimmer.

   Interestingly, if you turn the book 90 degrees, the effect is less powerful. This is because the brain interprets horizontal and vertical information in different ways.

HIDDEN CHANGES

TAKE A CAREFUL LOOK AT THIS GREEN SQUARE. Do you spot anything unusual about it, or is it simply a plain green square with a black cross drawn on top of it?

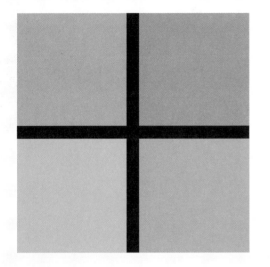

Surprisingly, you are actually looking at four different-colored squares! They are all shades of green, but they are more different than you might expect. With the thick black lines between the squares, you can't directly compare them, and your brain simply tells you that the square is a certain shade of green. It doesn't notice, or thinks it is unimportant to tell you, that these greens actually vary!

Here is the square without the black bars, so you can see how dissimilar the shades of green really are.

GRAY CONFUSION

THE TWO RED CIRCLES SHOW TWO DIFFERENT SHADES OF GRAY ... OR SO IT SEEMS. WHAT DO YOU THINK?

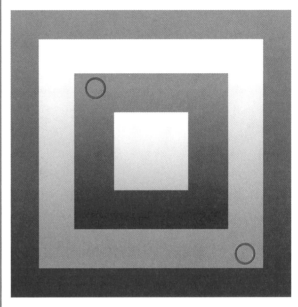

Amazingly, the two circles are actually indicating exactly the same shade of gray!

[BEHIND THE BRAIN]

The surrounding colors are dark at the bottom and bright at the top, which influences your perception. Also helping to confuse your brain are the smooth gradations in color between the top and bottom of the image, tricking you into thinking that there must be a stronger relationship between the top and bottom colors than there actually is.

COLOR LANGUAGES

If your perception of color is so variable, then how can you be sure that green is actually green, or red is really red? Have you ever disagreed with a friend or family member about the exact color of an item of clothing or some other object? The chances are that you have, and it's not just because the surrounding light and objects affect your interpretation. It's also because we all see color differently, based on our own unique experiences and physical differences.

Your experience of color is also influenced by the words you use to describe it. Many languages do not use separate words for "blue," "yellow," and "green" but instead include green within other colors, with one word that equates to "blue/green" and another that equates to "green/yellow." In this way, the concept of green itself as a separate color is simply not present. This might seem strange to you, because you think of them as very different colors. But someone who was brought up speaking a language that didn't distinguish them would not be used to thinking about these colors in the same way you do.

MIRROR, MIRROR ANSWERS PAGE 144

WHAT DO YOU THINK THESE PICTURES REPRESENT?

They might not be immediately recognizable, but if you rotate the page 90 degrees and look at it from the edge of the book, do you now have a possible idea?

These are, in fact, halves of symmetrical images. If you imagine a mirror running through the middle of each drawing, can you complete them? You can either do this in your head or by drawing on the paper, if you prefer. What other objects can you think of that are symmetrical, or can be drawn in a symmetrical way?

WARP FACTOR

WHAT DO YOU NOTICE ABOUT THESE TWO RED SQUARES, EACH DISPLAYED ON TOP OF BACKGROUND CIRCLES? Do they look like perfect squares, or do they appear to bend?

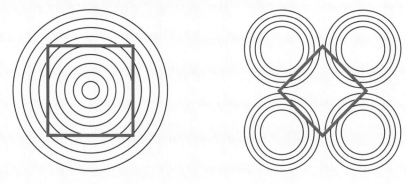

In fact, both red shapes are perfect squares. They only appear to bend because of the curved shapes beneath them, which confuse your brain into thinking that the straight lines passing over them must surely bend as well!

CAN YOU READ THIS?

WHAT DO YOU THINK THIS PICTURE IS DEPICTING? It looks a bit like a bar code, or perhaps some kind of secret message that would require a lot of practice to read.

In reality, you can read it without any special tools or skills. Can you figure out what it says? Make sure you look at it from every angle!

[BEHIND THE BRAIN]

The secret of this picture is to literally look at it from a different angle. Hold the book flat in front of you, so it is parallel to the ground, and look along the page at the text to the right. If you are holding it at the right angle, and if you are holding the book close enough, then the text should magically appear! The answer can be found at the bottom left corner of this page.

Of course, this isn't magic at all. It's simply that this text has been written far too tall to read from a normal viewpoint. When you view the page from a very sharp angle, however, it gets compressed in your vision. This corrects for the way it was stretched on the page, and you can finally read it!

IT SAYS "CONGRATULATIONS!"

SOUND AND VISION

HAVE YOU EVER WATCHED A MOVIE IN A THEATER AND FELT THE ROOM SHAKE FROM THE BASS OF AN EXPLOSION OR SOME OTHER LOUD NOISE?

The soundtrack to a movie is a hugely important part of what you are watching, which is not always obvious until you try watching the same scene again without any sound. Scary scenes are often much less scary without sound, and action scenes can seem boring without any noises.

But did you know that you can sometimes think you've heard a sound, just because what you're looking at is clearly something that should make a very loud or deep sound? This doesn't happen to everyone, but for some scenes in some movies, watching them even with the sound off leads some viewers to think they can hear the sound, even if it's just quietly and in the background.

We are so used to connecting what we see and what we hear that our brain makes connections between the two senses, even when there is none!

Try watching an action movie without the sound turned on. If you watch closely, can you still "hear" some of the effects?

TASTE AND SMELL

YOU MIGHT THINK THAT YOUR SENSE OF SMELL AND YOUR SENSE OF TASTE ARE VERY DIFFERENT, BUT IN FACT YOUR PERCEPTION OF TASTE IS HEAVILY INFLUENCED BY WHAT YOU CAN SMELL.

Have you ever noticed that when you have a cold, your food doesn't taste as good, or that it tastes different? That's because your sense of smell is impaired. Your tongue can taste only five distinct flavors, so what you think of as taste is in reality a combination of what you are smelling plus what

you can actually taste. Whether you like the taste of a food will also come down to more than just its flavor: the texture of the food, what it's like to chew and eat, and your own expectations of whether or not you will like it also influence how it tastes to you.

To test your sense of smell, try getting a friend to prepare a few different types of food for you—but without letting you see what they are. These can be simple things, such as a piece of apple or a piece of bread. It is best to chop them into small pieces so the texture doesn't give away what they are.

Once your friend is ready, close your eyes and hold your nose tight. Have your friend come into the room several times, each time with a different type of food they have prepared. Let them give you the food (perhaps placed on a spoon) to taste while you hold your nose, and think about what it tastes like. Then, let go of your nose and have your friend give you more of the same food to eat. Does it now taste different? And finally, open your eyes so you can see what it is and try again. Does it still taste the same?

THUNDER AND LIGHTNING

IF YOU SEE SOMEONE DROP A BOOK ON THE FLOOR, YOU WILL SEE THE BOOK HIT THE FLOOR AND HEAR IT HIT THE FLOOR AT THE SAME TIME. But when something happens farther away, you see it happen and hear the sound at different times. This is because the speed of sound and the speed of light are different. If there is a long pause between seeing something and hearing it, your brain doesn't necessarily realize that they are connected.

The best example of this is thunder and lightning. When you see lightning, you will usually hear thunder a certain amount of time afterward. But, unless you understand the science, you might not connect the two. The thunder is the sound the lightning made as it flashed through the air; the amount of time that passes between you seeing the lightning and you hearing the thunder will allow you to figure out how far away the lightning was: Roughly speaking, if you divide the number of seconds that pass by five, you can determine how many miles away the lightning was. Caution! Don't do fieldwork on this one: You should only watch storms (and do the math!) from a safe, indoor location.

WORD FIT ANSWERS PAGE 144

Place all of the words into the grid, one letter per box, so that every word can be found reading either across or down within the puzzle.

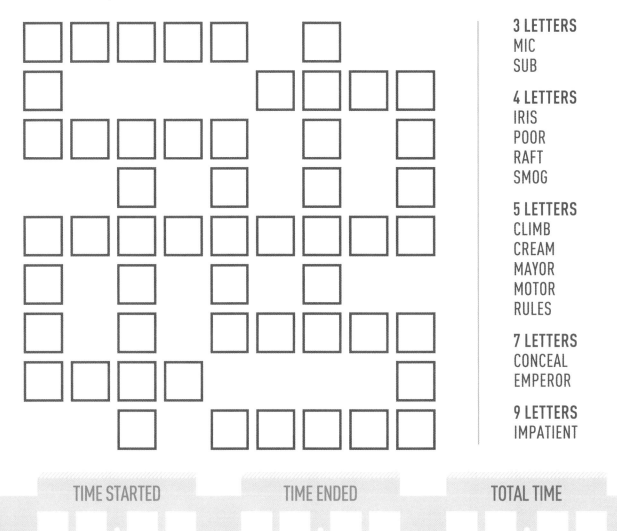

3 LETTERS
MIC
SUB

4 LETTERS
IRIS
POOR
RAFT
SMOG

5 LETTERS
CLIMB
CREAM
MAYOR
MOTOR
RULES

7 LETTERS
CONCEAL
EMPEROR

9 LETTERS
IMPATIENT

TIME STARTED

TIME ENDED

TOTAL TIME

A version of these puzzles will appear at the end of each chapter. After you solve them, record at the bottom of the page how long it took you to complete each puzzle. See if you can beat your own time as you work your way through chapter by chapter! You can use a timer or just consult a clock when you begin and when you finish.
→ **Are you ready to tackle some timed puzzles? Grab a pencil and start solving!**

BUILDING FENCES ANSWERS PAGE 144

Join all of the dots to draw a line that travels through every dot continuously and makes one single loop. To get you started, some dots have already been joined. You can use only horizontal and vertical lines to join dots, and the loop can't cross over itself or pass through any dot more than once.

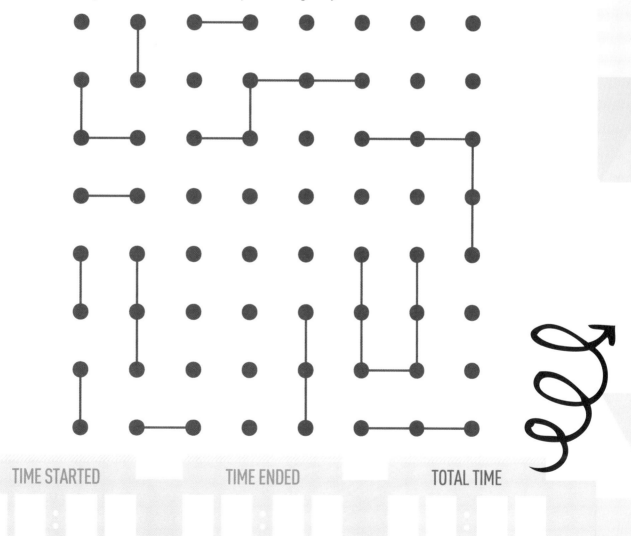

TIME STARTED   TIME ENDED   TOTAL TIME

ABC
1+2=3

CHAPTER THREE

WORDS AND LANGUAGE

Language is a big part of being human. From listening to the radio, to jotting down a note, to chatting with friends, we use language every day. It's how we communicate.

Some scientists believe humans are born wired for language: By the time they're born, babies can already tell the difference between their mother's language and a different one. Babies learn a language just by hearing people talk—no lessons required. And deaf children who aren't taught a formal sign language often invent their own. Language is very important to your brain: There are regions in every lobe involved with speaking and comprehending language. Are you ready to learn why your brain has a way with words?

$\longrightarrow$

ROUNDABOUT **WORD SEARCH**

ANSWERS PAGE 144

THIS WHOPPING WORD SEARCH IS HIDING THE NAMES OF 40 CIRCULAR OBJECTS. How many can you find in 10 minutes? Words can be written in any direction, including diagonally, and can be hidden either forward or backward.

```
                              N A G A E T T P Y S
                        B A W S O L L P P E O R L L B U
                    A N E R O H T O W I B L G C G P A A G E
                  Y P G U U D S O N L Z L A B T M T L T A E A
                P A A B R E S O S L E N Z L A G A D M C E H O E E B
              I E I E R B O O E E U Z R A A W W E C W T E A E L O E O
            S H I C A R B N N P H H S L O U M M H L M E L B I W E T L H
            B C M C E O T U I T Z O T H O E E A C E L L I A P L L O O A D
            R R O M H A E O O M L A M E A C N T U S E M E R T S E C U L S O
            H U E N R E R N D L A P B B A U H E B A I A A R L C M W R L R D O H
            L A N W H A B G B B B D O M D R C O D P I I N C D C A L T H K A T R I R B
            O B R H E E C A N R P P O T E L T T O B T K M L O E L C Z G L O B E S O
            O A I A E H R O A T A B E C A E D C E A Y R D L L N H E B P D G H A Y O Y O
            G N I R A N U W C B K R I P C E L U P O L F R E C O R D E L O W E E E O O U
            L E E H D O D A B E O T O O T E N L N N S N A L A C L I D N O E B L T D H P
            L M C M R K W L F A L E A V R O E N C E P B B I B R N W N L L L C V E N O E S P
            E H E T L E R N I T O E E L L A B L O W S C E N T C B U B T C H L A E S M O E M
            D C L O C K F A C E N R O R R E E Y E R N E E O R R N E A U A I Y P H R E E E M
            A N E N B W P E L I I L E L S I W R A C G C H P R T L E I O T R C C W S C R E E
            N M T L E A R Y O O I P A N C A K E H W A D T E O B A E P W E T O E W D C I B E
            L R E S E O L F E C Y O R C R O S I P E L R L T B R F D O H S P O G N P Z T N L
            R L S P A A A O Y T E N T R O O H E O T O L B R E H S A W C C I A N E S O T H T
            R C A H I R I W E M T U E R G A L N R A L R P R E A M A R B L E A A P P C N R Z
            C E T E N A T L I S N E E E C L H A L L L R E E E L C A L L N C R R P N T E Y O
            T W O R I L M A I H E L E P G O T D H Z C E T A L P A O T L P L W L E S S R S N
            K U E B R L R G G E R R O E O M E H A M B U R G E R D S W L E N T B K R C R
            O S E H C B U K G L R E T E O O C R M U E E N T T O A E T T A A E A C R I T
            O R N N A O A U A L C B L O L L C T E L B A T N R U T A M P I L A L B E N H
            A G Y D S O N L O E N N A C W A A G O D E O C A I N C E C H Z R H P T A
            L A M W O O T L O R O A L L I T R O T L O S I R N E R N P I C C C E C B
            G E A E T L L A E O O R A M N A B B R N E D B L E N R K E I Z T T O
            L S A R E E E V B A O R E D A S A L H G A E E O C B L E K S I D
            P L A N E T I C P H I I A A R E R Z B N A E L A R Z O M O E A
            I T N B B L A T L I T K E S N C R R L H H L R R E T R T E C
            O E I W T R D E K N O O H I H S R E A H O W G U A C M L
              B C O P S C G O B O L R E R E B I L C O A B L A C B
                O C Z I H T A C C Y O L M L A R R H N E I H
                  P C C B D C L A E E H N I I T P O O H O
                    N U E E O D E L C B E R N A O N
                        K R R E C U A S L T
```

BAGEL	CIRCLE	HAMBURGER	ORANGE	RECORD	TIRE
BALL	CLOCK FACE	HOOP	PAIL	RING	TORTILLA
BARREL	COIN	MANHOLE	PANCAKE	SAUCER	TURNTABLE
BOTTLE TOP	COOKIE	COVER	PEARL	SCREW HEAD	WASHER
BOWL	DOUGHNUT	MARBLE	PIZZA	SINK DRAIN	WHEEL
BRACELET	GLOBE	MEDAL	PLANET	SPHERE	YO-YO
BUTTON	HALO	MOON	PLATE	THE SUN	

WORD PLAY

DOES THE LANGUAGE YOU SPEAK CHANGE THE WAY YOU THINK? IT SEEMS IMPOSSIBLE—WORDS ARE JUST HOW WE EXPRESS THE THOUGHTS IN OUR HEADS, RIGHT? SCIENTISTS AREN'T SO SURE.

SUPER SENSES

English speakers use the word "it" to refer to any kind of object, from a broom to a bus. But in many other languages, such as Spanish and German, speakers don't use "it." In those languages, every object has a gender.

In Spanish, bridges, clocks, forks, newspapers, the sun, and love are all masculine. In German, those same words are all feminine. So Germans refer to a bridge as "she," and Spaniards call it "he." This difference made language researchers curious, so they asked Spanish and German speakers to grade objects on a range of traits. They found that Spanish speakers were more likely to say bridges, clocks, and forks have characteristics often associated with masculinity, like "strength." German speakers were more likely to use words traditionally associated with femininity, like "elegant." This hints that the language we use to discuss the world around us shapes the way we understand that world.

DIRECTIONAL DIFFERENCES

If you're giving someone directions in English, you might say something like, "After you enter the building, turn right, go down the hall, and open the third door on your left." But a speaker of an Australian Aboriginal language called Guugu Yimithirr would give these directions differently. Speakers of this language, and several others around the world, use directions like "north" and "south" instead of words like "left" or "right." A Guugu Yimithirr speaker might ask you to "scoot your chair to the south" or "raise your north hand and move your south leg eastward."

This way of explaining location is confusing to people who don't speak Guugu Yimithirr and languages like it. These speakers have to know where the cardinal directions are at every moment, using a mental compass.

BILINGUAL BRAINPOWER

Between 60 and 75 percent of people worldwide speak at least two languages. Scientists believe the ability to speak multiple languages might do more for you than helping you read a menu in a foreign country. Research has hinted that speaking multiple languages strengthens the brain: Bilingual speakers, for example, seem to be better at focusing and solving problems. And some studies have shown that they can even recover faster from brain injuries, such as strokes.

THERE ARE ABOUT **7,000** DIFFERENT **LANGUAGES** SPOKEN AROUND THE **WORLD** TODAY.

Hello!

MEXICAN WOMAN MAKING BREAD

GUUGU YIMITHIRR MEN HAVING A CONVERSATION

If they don't, they can't understand what people around them are saying! Speakers of these languages have to develop an incredibly sharp sense of direction. In one case, a speaker of the southern Mexican language Tzeltal was blindfolded and spun around more than 20 times. While dizzy and still blindfolded, he could point out the cardinal directions with no trouble.

MOST PEOPLE **PROCESS** LANGUAGE IN THE **DOMINANT** HALF OF **THEIR BRAIN.** IF YOU'RE **RIGHT-HANDED,** THAT'S YOUR **LEFT HALF.**

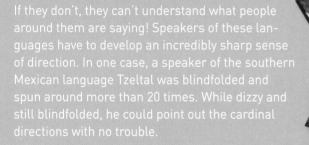
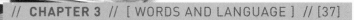

MULTI-ANAGRAMS ANSWERS PAGE 144

AN ANAGRAM IS A WORD THAT IS MADE UP OF THE SAME LETTERS AS ANOTHER WORD, but in a different order. For example, LEMON is an anagram of MELON, because the *L* and the *M* have swapped places. ELMNO is also an anagram of MELON, even though it's a less interesting one because it isn't an actual word.

Each of the following sets of letters is special, because they can be anagrammed to make three or more words. For example, AER can be anagrammed to make ARE, EAR, and ERA. For each set, see if you can find the suggested number of anagrams:

3 WORDS:
N W O
ANSWER →

3 WORDS:
T R A
ANSWER →

3 WORDS:
E T A
ANSWER →

3 WORDS:
A P S W
ANSWER →

4 WORDS:
A N P S
ANSWER →

5 WORDS:
O P S T
ANSWER →

YESSS!!!

THEMED ANAGRAM SETS

ANSWERS PAGE 144

CAN YOU UNSCRAMBLE EACH WORD IN THESE TWO LISTS TO REVEAL EITHER A FRUIT OR AN ANIMAL?
Ignore any spaces in the anagrams: They're just there to make it trickier!

FRUITS

Cheap _____

An ogre _____

Lump _____

Among _____

Mile _____

Starry brew _____

Pager _____

Pipe panel _____

Rat engine _____

ANIMALS

Shore _____

Nails _____

Toga _____

Sneak _____

Lino _____

Flow _____

Low _____

Tab _____

The arms _____

[BEHIND THE BRAIN]

Were the anagrams harder than you thought they might be? If so, there's a good explanation: Your brain remembers the words you've learned based on their first letter, so when the first letter of a word is wrong you find it much more difficult to figure it out. It's also why you sometimes experience the "tip of the tongue" effect, when you think you know the first letter of a word or name, but you can't remember the rest of it.

WORD PYRAMID

ANSWERS PAGE 144

CAN YOU WRITE A LETTER IN EACH SQUARE OF THIS WORD PYRAMID SO THAT EACH ROW SPELLS OUT A DIFFERENT WORD THAT MATCHES ITS CLUE? Each row will contain the same letters as the row above plus one extra, although the letters might need to be rearranged to make the new word. For example, DOG on the top row might have *L* added, then the letters rearranged to make GOLD. Next, it might have an *E* added and the letters rearranged to make LODGE.

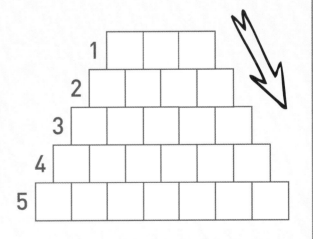

Clues:
1) Common family pet (Hint: not a dog!)
2) Something that is true about the world
3) A type of art, such as paper-folding or model-making
4) A number that divides into another number
5) A place where goods are made

WORD RIDDLES ANSWERS PAGE 144

CAN YOU FIND THE ANSWER TO EACH OF THESE CRAFTY WORD RIDDLES? Solve them by thinking about the letters that make up the words, rather than the exact meaning of each word. For example, the answer to the riddle "What word becomes longer when you remove a letter from it?" is "lounger," because when you remove the letter *u* you get "longer"!

What occurs once in a minute, twice in a week, but never in a month?

ANSWER →

In what book does "first" always come before "second" and "second" come before "third" but "fifth" always comes before them all?

ANSWER →

Which word in this sentence is misspelled?

ANSWER →

CODE-CRACKING I

ANSWERS PAGE 144

CAN YOU USE YOUR SKILLS AND INTUITION TO CRACK THE CODE BEING USED HERE AND FIGURE OUT WHAT EACH OF THESE WELL-KNOWN EXPRESSIONS SHOULD SAY? The words and letters are all correct, but they're not in the correct order.

HINT: If you get stuck, try looking at these sentences in a different way.

TON'D TOUNC ROUY SHICKENC EEFORB YHET HATCH

ANSWER →

ENCO NI A ELUB NOOM

ANSWER →

A GLESSINB NI EISGUISD

ANSWER →

CODE-CRACKING II

ANSWERS PAGE 144

HERE'S ANOTHER SECRET CODE, BUT THIS ONE'S A BIT TRICKIER. Every letter in the alphabet has been changed to the one after it, so A is written as B, and B is written as C, and so on.

BU UIF ESPQ PG B IBU

ANSWER →

TJU PO UIF GFODF

ANSWER →

BDUJPOT TQFBL MPVEFS UIBO XPSET

ANSWER →

REVEAL THE PHRASE

ANSWERS PAGE 144

SOME WELL-KNOWN PHRASES HAVE BEEN DISGUISED BY WRITING THEM IN A WAY THAT REPRESENTS THE WORDS VISUALLY, instead of writing out the actual phrases. For example, the first picture below represents the phrase "Time after time," because you see the word "time" written after the word "time." See if you can figure out the rest:

CLASSIC CROSSWORD
ANSWERS PAGE 144

GIVE THIS CROSSWORD PUZZLE A GO BY SOLVING THE ACROSS AND DOWN CLUES. The answer to each "across" clue should be written from left to right, one letter per square, and starting at the number that matches the clue. Down answers work the same, except that you should write them from top to bottom.

Some clues are trickier than others, so if you're stuck on a clue, try another one and come back to it later. As you add letters to the grid, it will help you solve the other clues, too.

BONUS! Some squares are colored yellow. Once you complete the puzzle, read these from left to right, row by row, to spell out two words that represent something this chapter is full of!

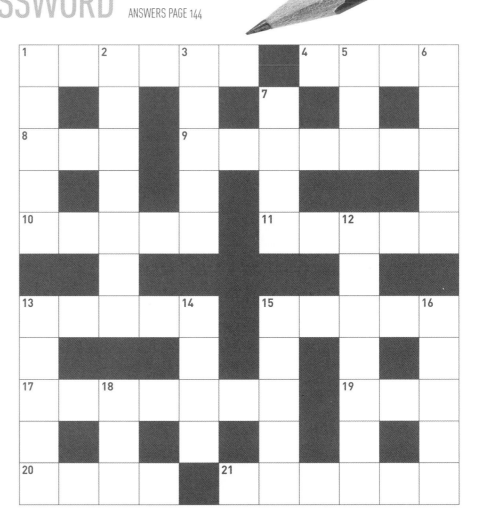

Across
1. A period of 60 seconds (6)
4. Medicine (4)
8. An even number just less than three (3)
9. Speak softly (7)
10. You might use this for drawing straight lines (5)
11. Windows are made of this (5)
13. Not very nice at all (5)
15. Long, narrow tube for drinking (5)
17. A common taste for white ice cream (7)
19. Bird with a nighttime hoot (3)
20. Limbs that you use for walking (4)
21. Social media post about yourself, or the current state of things (6)

Down
1. A machine that powers moving vehicles (5)
2. Thin pasta strips, often used in Asian food (7)
3. A tall building, such as a skyscraper (5)
5. Tear something, such as a piece of paper (3)
6. Female children; not boys but _____ (5)
7. The part of a bird used for flying (4)
12. Place where planes take off and land (7)
13. Book containing a fictional story (5)
14. Yellow part of an egg (4)
15. Clever, intelligent (5)
16. The vertical sides of a room (5)
18. Repeatedly pester someone (3)

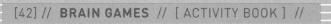

ARROW WORD ANSWERS PAGE 144

IN THIS CROSSWORD, ALL OF THE CLUES ARE GIVEN INSIDE THE GRID. Each clue has an arrow showing where to write the answer. Just start at the square with the arrow and then continue in the direction it points. One clue is already solved, to show you how it works.

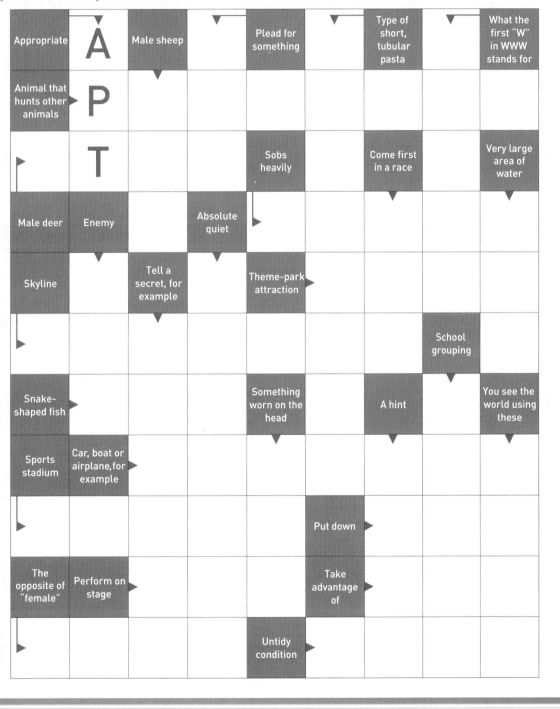

A–Z CROSSWORD ANSWERS PAGE 145

CAN YOU COMPLETE THIS PARTIALLY SOLVED CROSSWORD GRID? ONE OF EACH LETTER, FROM A TO Z, IS MISSING.
It's up to you to figure out where each letter goes. Be careful, however, because although there may be more than one way of completing some of the words, there's only one way that uses all 26 letters of the alphabet only once. Start by placing letters that you are sure of, skipping over squares where multiple letters can fit.

CROSS OFF THE LETTERS AS YOU PLACE THEM, USING THIS HANDY ALPHABET: A B C D E F G H I J K L M N O P Q R S T U V W X Y Z

SPIRAL CROSSWORD

ANSWERS PAGE 145

HERE'S A VERY UNUSUAL CROSSWORD THAT YOU PROBABLY HAVEN'T SEEN BEFORE! IN THIS PUZZLE, instead of writing clues across and down, you now need to write them inward (clockwise) and outward (counterclockwise).

Just like a normal crossword, you solve each clue and write the answer in the grid, one letter per box. But in this puzzle, the boxes are arranged in a spiral. As before, if you get stuck, skip to another clue: There's a good chance the clue reading in the opposite direction will give you a hint.

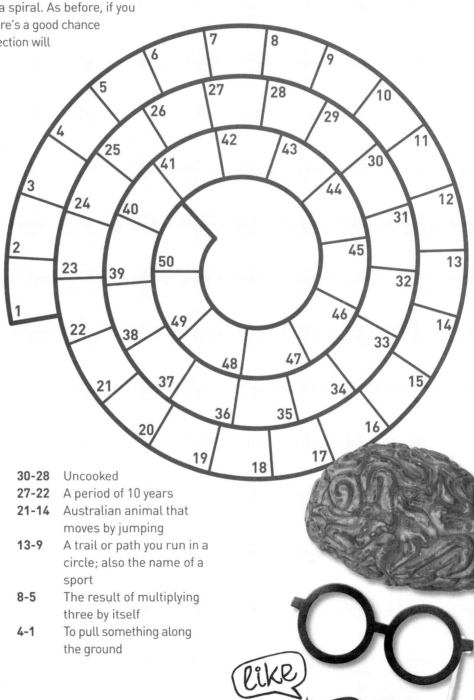

Inward

1-6   Outdoor place where you plant flowers

7-9   Something a squid shoots out; also what comes out of a pen

10-12   A vehicle you travel around in

13-15   Also; as well

16-18   A piece of cloth you use to clean with

19-23   Without any clothes on

24-26   A value of playing card; also an expert

27-31   One of Snow White's helpers

32-34   Not thin

35-39   Clever; intelligent

40-42   Rest on a chair; to not stand

43-50   Device used to heat a room; also an engine-cooling device in a car

Outward

50-48   Turn bad, like fruit does

47-45   Assistance or help; first ____

44-39   A painter, sculptor, or other creative person

38-36   Male sheep

35-31   People who work for an organization; also a long stick used while walking

30-28   Uncooked

27-22   A period of 10 years

21-14   Australian animal that moves by jumping

13-9   A trail or path you run in a circle; also the name of a sport

8-5   The result of multiplying three by itself

4-1   To pull something along the ground

like

ANSWERS PAGE 145

EVEN IF YOU'VE ACED ALL OF THE PREVIOUS WORD SEARCH CHALLENGES IN THIS CHAPTER, here's a puzzle that is sure to put your puzzle-solving skills to the test!

There are three word searches shown here, each with a different topic: flowers, colors, and names. Sound simple? Well, all of the words in our word bank have been mixed up together, and there are some words that have multiple meanings and could therefore be found in more than one word search. For example, ROSE is a flower, but it's also a color, and it's even a name—so you'd need to check all three word searches until you found the right place for it!

HINT: Each word appears in only one puzzle, and each word search contains 16 words. (There are a total of 48 words in the word bank: 16×3=48.) So keep track of how many words you've found in each puzzle; once you've found 16 you can stop searching within that particular word search. Remember, some words appear backward.

WORD BANK

AMBER	BLACK
ANEMONE	BLUE
ASH	BROWN
ASTER	BUTTERCUP
AZALEA	CARNATION
BEGONIA	CRIMSON

FLOWERS

```
D E E C A R N A T I O N F I I
A D O V E N U R T O H O M D T
F L U D O G S N O W D R O P A
F O D R O L O R D I H C R O E
O G B R L N G R H A G S O U E
D I T U B A O X E A U P S A V
I R L R T R V G O N A N O E P
L A F O E T A E F F O S A N O
S M E T D I E L N P R T N O O
N R S U S I O R E D O V T M L
F A O H L W E T C A E N U E E
N A C O E U U U N U W R L N L
P U B R A N I A O I P S I A P
F O A C I A I N O G E B P V D
N O G A R D P A N S X R N W I
```

CYAN GREEN LIAM NOAH POPPY SNOWDROP
DAFFODIL HAZEL LILAC OLIVE ROSE SUNFLOWER
DAISY INDIGO LILY ORANGE RUBY TULIP
FOXGLOVE IRIS MAGENTA ORCHID SAFFRON VIOLET
FUCHSIA JADE MARIGOLD PETUNIA SILVER WHITE
GRAY LAVENDER MASON PINK SNAPDRAGON YELLOW

COLORS

```
S N C O L S I N E E R G E N I
W I B R E V L I S W B S N A O
O N N A Y R B A R B E U E K L
L R L N T N F N L I K E S V G
L N I O O N A U K C A L B C W
E E M R G R E Y E I N D I G O
Y O K F L G Y G C L B O O G Y
N N R F L B N R A C L E G O L
W R C A M A C G R M T G P L O
O K W S R E W I Y I T I E N L
R P A O N G M R H B N A I C S
B A G E P S R W E K N N K O A
A V G R O R I O R G G N C A I
N O E N E B L N N G R A Y I H
I B C A L I L E H S C Y E E R
```

NAMES

```
A M H E P E A E M L B E O A A
A I A O L E A Y A A S I S I D
P D Z I D B E L E M I A U E R
D V E L A A Y S I A D L P B I
E L L I A I L E Z A L M A H O
A E L A Z A V R O P E L H S S
S J A H B I R E B M A A I R E
N V I O L E T P A J A D E L L
H S A O P Z S R Y I I E R I I
A L V I V O A L A O R Y L I S
T E R R E M P I S A I Y H D H
A L U Z O Y A P L M S A H L A
D A B N L S O S Y S O R V E A
E E Y A S T E O O N E S P Z S
E O U V Y P L V U N E A O A S
```

WORDS AND LANGUAGE → WORD PROPERTIES

REVERSIBLE WORDS ANSWERS PAGE 145

SOME WORDS ARE MIRROR IMAGES OF EACH OTHER. That is, they make sense read both forward and backward. For example, when you read the word DESSERTS backward it becomes STRESSED.

See if you can figure out the pairs of words below from the given clues. Remember: The words will be mirror images of each other!

A treat that recognizes an achievement   ANSWER →
A compartment you slide out of a desk or dresser

To catch in a cage   ANSWER →
A section of something

Having given back money that was owed   ANSWER →
A baby's "underwear"

Utensil you eat your cereal with (plural!)   ANSWER →
People who spy on other people

PALINDROMIC WORDS ANSWERS PAGE 145

A PALINDROME IS A WORD OR PHRASE THAT READS THE SAME BACKWARD AS IT DOES FORWARD. For example, "MADAM, I'M ADAM" is a very famous palindrome—notice how the letters reading up to the *I* in the middle are the same as those from the end to the middle.

There are a small number of English words that are palindromes, all on their own. An example is DEIFIED, which means "worshipped as a god." See if you can figure out the following palindromes, all of which are single words:

__ __ __ **A female sheep**

__ __ __ **A young dog**

__ __ __ __ **The middle of the day**

__ __ __ __ __ __ **Completely flat and even**

__ __ __ __ __ __ **Helicopter blade**

__ __ __ __ __ __ **Individual performances, such as when singing**

MOM!

ZIGZAG

ANSWERS PAGE 145

YOUR AIM IN THIS PUZZLE IS TO WRITE A LETTER IN EACH EMPTY BOX, so that every row contains a seven-letter word. Boxes linked by the gray bars should contain the same letters, so the two letters you write on the end of the first row should be added to the start of the second row. Copy the letters in exactly the same order.

It is best to start at the top and work your way down, but if you get stuck you could try starting at the bottom and working your way up!

| E | A | R | L | O | | |

| | | A | N | B | | |

| | | A | I | N | | |

| | | O | M | A | | |

| | | E | A | T | | |

| | | U | P | T | | |

| | | I | T | I | O | N |

WORD SQUARE

ANSWERS PAGE 145

HOW MANY WORDS OF THREE OR MORE LETTERS CAN YOU FIND IN THIS WORD SQUARE? To form a word, start on any letter and then follow a path from letter to letter, moving only to a touching letter at each point. Diagonal moves are allowed, but you can't double back or reuse a letter within a word.

TARGETS: 15 words is good, 25 is fantastic, and 35 is amazing!

BONUS! There is one word that uses all nine letters—can you find it?

U	C	A
D	E	T
N	O	I

ANSWER →

WORD MASH-UP

ANSWERS PAGE 145

IN THIS EXERCISE, TWO WORDS HAVE BEEN SMOOSHED TOGETHER, but the letters of each word in each pair are still in the correct order. For example, "WAIT and SEE" could be written as WASIETE, or as WSEEAIT, or various other ways. The word that comes first in the phrase always has the first letter in the mash-up, as in the example above.

Colors: BWLAHICTKE
ANSWER →

Fruit: APOPLRANEGESS
ANSWER →

Board game: CLHUADTEDESRS
ANSWER →

Text editing: CPUASTTE
ANSWER →

Flag: SKCRUOSSLBOLNES
ANSWER →

WORD SLIDER ANSWERS PAGE 145

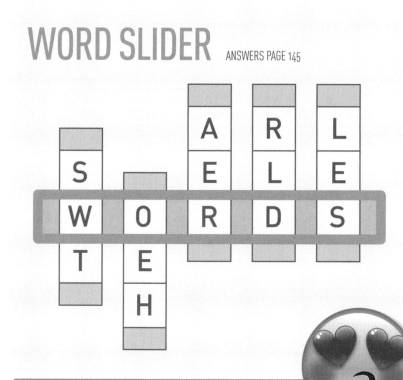

HOW MANY WORDS CAN YOU MAKE USING THIS WORD SLIDER? It consists of five strips, each with three letters. Imagine sliding each strip up and down to make different words. One is made for you, to show how it works.

How many more words can you find? 5 is good, 10 is fantastic, and 15 is amazing!

ANSWER →

HIDDEN WORDS ANSWERS PAGE 146

CAN YOU FIND A HIDDEN ANIMAL IN EACH OF THESE SOMETIMES SILLY PHRASES AND SENTENCES? For example, "Came later" hides a camel: "**Came l**ater."

A billionaire ANSWER →

The yeti gerbil ANSWER →

My robe arrived. ANSWER →

Just a mo—username not found! ANSWER →

To-and-fro go the children. ANSWER →

Fish or seal? ANSWER →

STAR POWER WORD SEARCH

ANSWERS PAGE 146

CAN YOU FIND ALL OF THESE "STARRY" ENTRIES IN THE WORD SEARCH? Wherever the word STAR is found inside a word, you should look for a picture of a star instead of the four letters. For example, if you were searching for COSTAR, then you would actually search for CO instead. You should also look for STAR across multiword phrases: So instead of REST AREA, you would look for RE EA.

ALL-STAR
COSTA RICA
CUSTARD
DASTARDLY
DEATH STAR
DWARF STAR

FALSE START
GOLD STAR
KICK START
LONE STAR STATE
MEGASTAR
MOVIE STAR

NONSTARTER
OUTSTARE
RESTARTED
ROCK STAR
SHOOTING STAR
STARBOARD

STARCH
STARDOM
STARLET
UPSTART

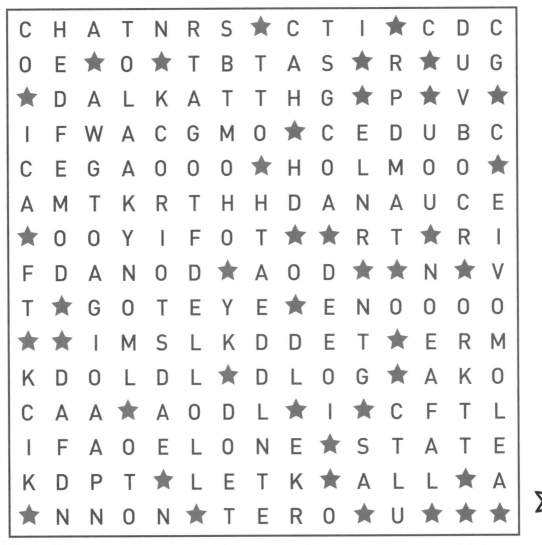

NUMBER CRUNCHING

ANSWERS PAGE 146

THERE IS SOMETHING SNEAKY GOING ON IN THIS ORDINARY-LOOKING WORD SEARCH. If you look closely at the words in the word bank, you'll notice that each has a "number" inside it. ANCIENT WORLD, for example, is hiding TWO, and CLONES is hiding ONE. To find the word in the word search, you'll need to remove the number from the inside and find what remains. So, for example, instead of ANCIENT WORLD, you would look for ANCIENRLD—that is, without the TWO that's hidden inside. Or instead of CLONES, you'd look for CLS—without the ONE. Beware: A couple of entries have more than one number hidden inside them!

ANCIENT WORLD	FREIGHTED
ARTWORK	NONEXISTENT
BREAKS EVEN	SUNNINESS
CANINES	SWEET SIXTEEN
CLONES	TAKE FIVE
CONDITIONER	TENSIONER
FEMININE	THREE WISE MEN
FOOTWORK	UNDERWEIGHT
FOURTH OF JULY	VERMILLION

```
W D S D K R I T I D N O C F T
L O B W R T R E I S S I D H I
E U W I E R R E W G I K X Y U
W N N V D E B R E A K I S L W
O D T E C L T N U N E A H U E
I E R R M I R T A W N U H J F
K R R R S E R N E S A C H F G
E W C A I R S F E E K A T O S
A F E M I S Y I S I J R O H N
T N N W I S N L W E C A K T I
L I L Y R F O O R K S N R N T
D A K R K R R A W I W S A N R
E U R R R C I U D N R I A H U
R A R E E E L R S R H Y W H R
F R S S N U S S T S I X N E O
```

WORD NET

ANSWERS PAGE 146

CAN YOU FIND THE WORD "SECRET" HIDDEN INSIDE THIS NETWORK OF LETTERS? Start on any circle with an *S* on it, then try to spell the rest of the word by following along the lines to connected letters—without jumping over any circles.

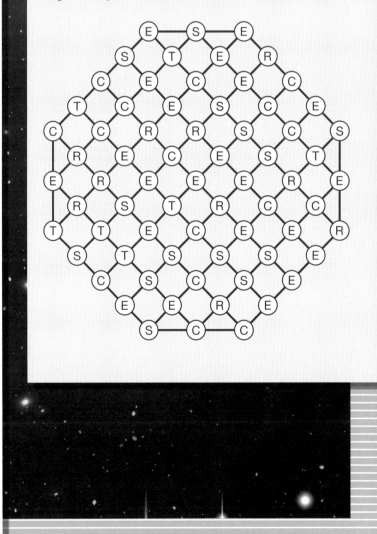

WORD FIT ANSWERS PAGE 146

Place all of the words into the grid, one letter per box, so that every word can be found reading either across or down within the puzzle.

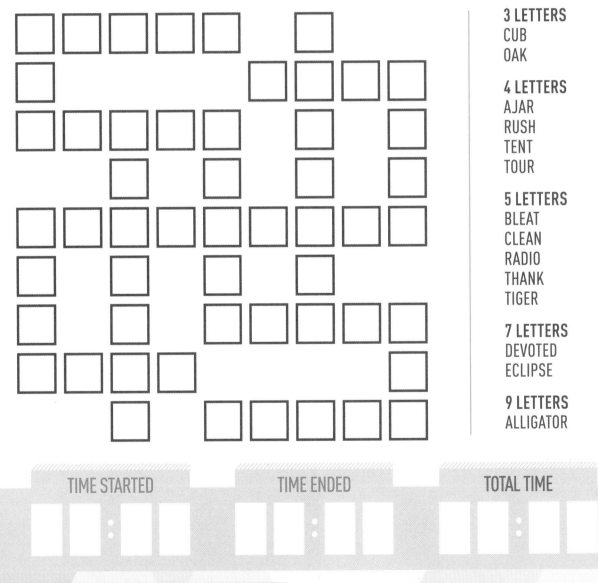

3 LETTERS
CUB
OAK

4 LETTERS
AJAR
RUSH
TENT
TOUR

5 LETTERS
BLEAT
CLEAN
RADIO
THANK
TIGER

7 LETTERS
DEVOTED
ECLIPSE

9 LETTERS
ALLIGATOR

TIME STARTED   TIME ENDED   TOTAL TIME

BUILDING FENCES ANSWERS PAGE 146

Join all the dots to draw a line that travels through every dot continuously and makes one single loop. To get you started, some dots have already been joined. You can use only horizontal and vertical lines to join dots, and the loop can't cross over itself or use any dot more than once.

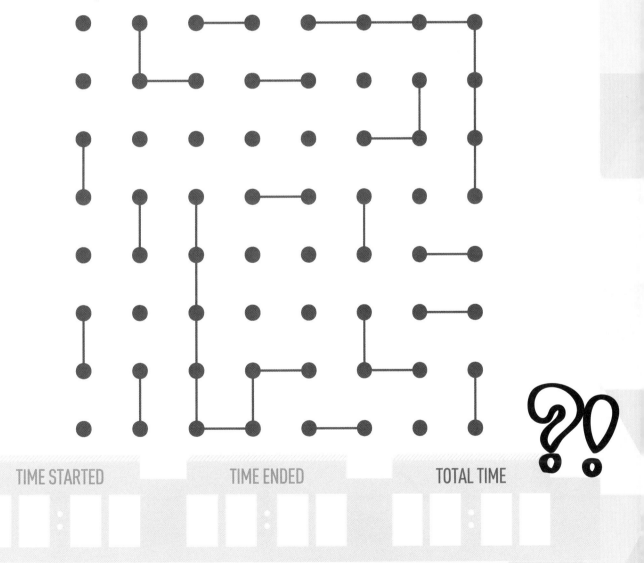

TIME STARTED	TIME ENDED	TOTAL TIME

CHAPTER **FOUR**
SPATIAL SMARTS

In school, you sharpen your smarts by writing reports and solving math problems. But there are some types of intelligence that aren't covered in the classroom. You rely on your spatial skills to help you navigate through everyday life—from using a map, to putting together a puzzle, to packing a suitcase.

Many different careers rely on spatial intelligence. Astronomers use it to visualize how planets move through space. Engineers use it to make sense of how the parts of a machine work together. Doctors use it to interpret x-ray images. Give your spatial skills a test with the puzzles in this chapter, and maybe you'll decide to join these careers some day!

→

REFLECTED CLOCKS

ANSWERS PAGE 146

THE FOLLOWING ANALOG AND DIGITAL CLOCKS HAVE BEEN REFLECTED IN A MIRROR. Write down the time that was shown on each clock before it was reflected. It might be trickier than you expect!

1

ANSWER →

2

ANSWER →

3

ANSWER →

4

ANSWER →

5

ANSWER →

6

ANSWER →

WHERE'S MY CLASSROOM?

ON YOUR FIRST DAY AT A NEW SCHOOL, EVERYTHING LOOKS UNFAMILIAR. YOU DON'T KNOW WHERE THE CAFETERIA IS, AND YOU GET LOST LOOKING FOR THE BATHROOM. BUT A FEW WEEKS LATER, YOU CAN WALK FROM THE GYM TO THE SCIENCE LAB WITHOUT EVEN THINKING ABOUT IT. HOW DOES YOUR BRAIN MAKE SENSE OF YOUR SPACE?

MAKING MAPS

Recently, scientists have begun to unravel the mystery. They recorded the activity of individual neurons in the hippocampus, or memory center, of a rat's brain. As the rat explored an enclosure looking for food, the researchers saw that whenever the rat entered specific parts of the enclosure, some particular neurons would send blips of electricity to the rest of the brain. Different neurons were responsible for letting the brain know when the rat hit certain spots. These neurons were all working together to create a map of the rat's surroundings.

Scientists now think that these mapmaking cells, called place cells, are how your brain tells you where you are. The human brain has place cells, too—they help us find our car in a parking garage or our classroom on a school campus.

GET LOST

We all know somebody who always seems to get lost—maybe this person is even you! Spatial skills vary widely from one person to the next. But some people with a rare brain condition have so much trouble with navigation they can even get lost inside their own houses.

SOME **BOARD GAMES,** LIKE **CHESS,** REQUIRE **SPATIAL SMARTS:** PLAYERS HAVE TO VISUALIZE IN THEIR MIND HOW THE BOARD WILL **LOOK** AFTER MULTIPLE MOVES.

In 2008, scientists identified the first recorded case of developmental topographical disorientation, or DTD. People with DTD have brains that look perfectly normal. But they never develop navigational abilities. Many report that they have to rely on friends to drive them around and that they forget how to find particular rooms in familiar places, such as their homes.

Scientists believe this condition happens when different parts of the brain involved in navigation—like the hippocampus, the part that remembers where locations are, and the frontal cortex, the part that figures out how to get there—don't work together very well. Some researchers think the same idea might explain why reading maps is a snap for some people and a tough task for others: One study found that people with higher levels of connectivity between brain regions tended to be better at navigating through a virtual world.

YOUR BRAIN ON GPS

Not so long ago, people had to pull out paper maps to find their way around new locations. But in the modern world, getting around an unfamiliar area is a lot easier: Many people have their smartphones read out step-by-step directions. That made one team of scientists from University College London wonder: How is GPS affecting our spatial smarts?

In a 2017 study, the team enlisted volunteers to virtually navigate an area of London while inside an fMRI brain-scanning machine. Some were fed turn-by-turn directions, while others had to find their own way around. The people who had to devise their own route showed spikes of activity in their brain's hippocampus and frontal cortex. But the brains of those using a GPS were silent in those areas! So if you want to keep your spatial skills sharp, try shutting off your GPS and finding your own way from time to time.

ROTATED SHAPES ANSWERS PAGE 146

WHICH OF THE FOUR IMAGES ON THE RIGHT OF EACH PUZZLE IS EXACTLY THE SAME AS THE IMAGE ON THE LEFT, except for being rotated?

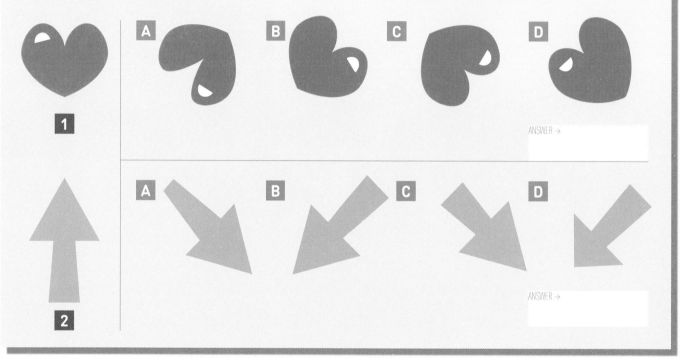

ANSWER →

ANSWER →

ROTATE THE IMAGE ANSWERS PAGE 146

CAN YOU COPY ALL THE LINES AND CIRCLES FROM THE LEFT-HAND IMAGE OVER ONTO THE RIGHT-HAND IMAGE? Once you add them to the lines and circles on the right, you will have formed a simple picture. **BUT HERE'S THE TRICKY PART:** The grid on the right-hand side has been rotated 90 degrees clockwise, compared to the grid on the left. The colored dots are in the same positions in each picture, to help show how this works, and there is a bold red dot in the same corner of each picture. This means that you must rotate the lines and shapes as you copy them. Good luck!

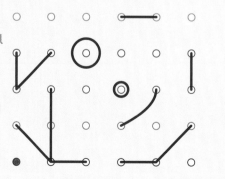

FIND THE MATCHING PAIR

ANSWERS PAGE 146

THESE IMAGES OF THE STATUE OF LIBERTY ALL LOOK VERY SIMILAR, but there are some small differences among them. Only two are identical to each other. Can you find this identical pair? The images have been rotated, to make it trickier.

A
B

C
D

E
F

ANSWER →

FOLDING IN HALF

ANSWERS PAGE 147

TAKE A LOOK AT THE CIRCLE AND THE STAR BELOW. Imagine that each of these images is drawn on see-through paper, so that when it is folded in half you can see both sides at once.
If each image were folded along the dashed line, which of the four images below would be the result?

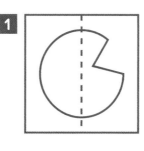

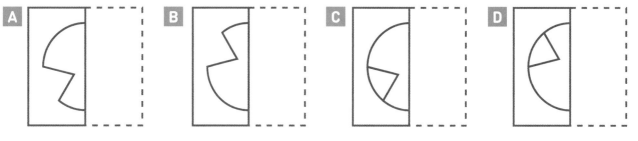

ANSWER →

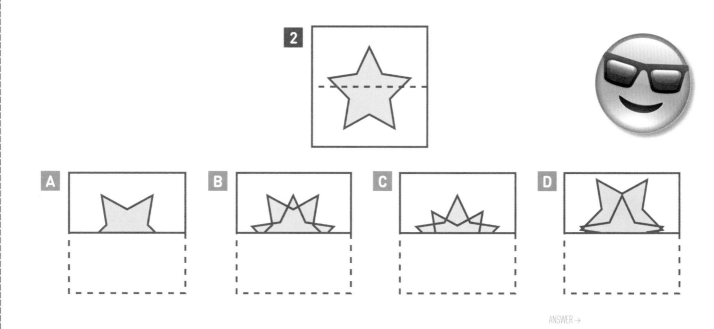

ANSWER →

FOLDING AND PUNCHING ANSWERS PAGE 147

IMAGINE FOLDING THE PIECE OF PAPER SHOWN AT THE TOP LEFT OF EACH PUZZLE IN THE WAY SHOWN BY THE WHITE ARROWS. Then, once the paper is folded, you punch the white holes as marked. Next, you fully unfold the paper. Which of the four images below would be the result?

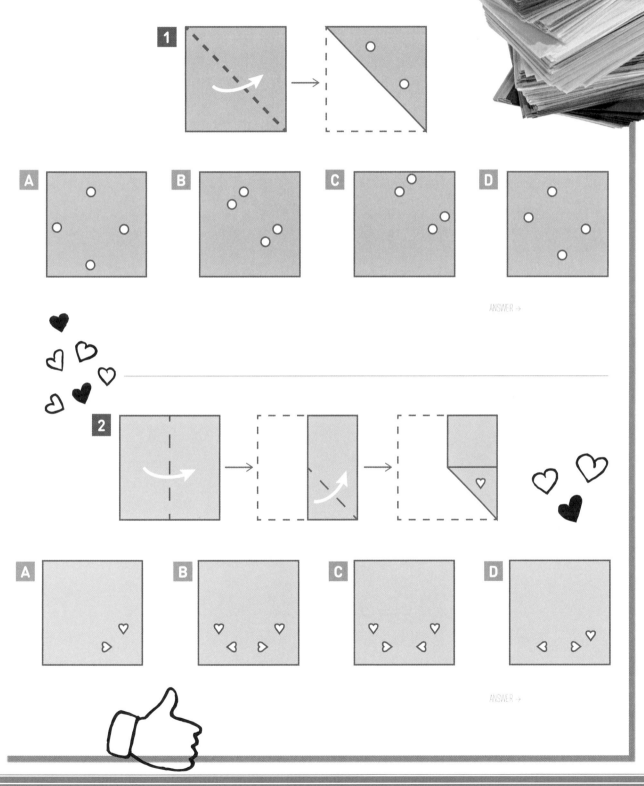

ANSWER →

ANSWER →

SILHOUETTES ANSWERS PAGE 147

WHICH OF THE FOUR SILHOUETTES EXACTLY MATCHES the outline of the top of the Empire State Building, as shown at the top of the page?

A

B

C

D

ANSWER →

SPOT THE INVERSE

ANSWERS PAGE 147

TO INVERT AN IMAGE, you swap the colors so that black becomes white and white becomes black. Which of these white buildings is the exact inverse of the black building?

A

B

C

ANSWER →

INVERSE GRIDS

ANSWERS PAGE 147

IN THIS PUZZLE, your challenge is to copy the upper blue-and-orange grid onto the top five rows of the larger center grid, and the lower blue-and-orange grid onto the bottom five rows of the larger grid. Sound easy? Not so fast! You must invert the blue and orange, so that you copy the blue squares as orange, and the orange squares as blue. The result will be a simple picture.

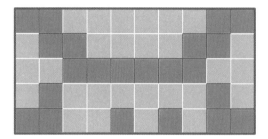

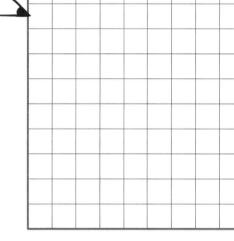

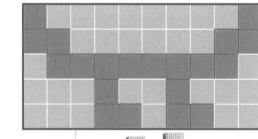

OVER AND UNDER MAP

ANSWERS PAGE 147

BEGINNING AT START, where do you end up when following each of these sets of instructions to travel along this road layout? An intersection is a point where two or more lines come together.

MAP ONE

1. Begin at START.
2. Head south to the intersection.
3. Head west, and then go south and stop at the first intersection.
4. Head east, and then go south at the third intersection.
5. At the next intersection, turn east and follow the path around to the four-way intersection.
6. Head west, cross over one intersection and then head south.

AT WHICH LETTER DO YOU END UP?

ANSWER →

MAP TWO

1. Begin at START.
2. Turning as soon as you can, head east, south, west, south, west, and north.
3. Head east, crossing one intersection before turning south.
4. At the next intersection, head west as far as you can go, then turn south and follow the path around to the first intersection you reach.
5. Cross over that intersection, and then two more intersections, before turning south.

AT WHICH LETTER DO YOU END UP?

ANSWER →

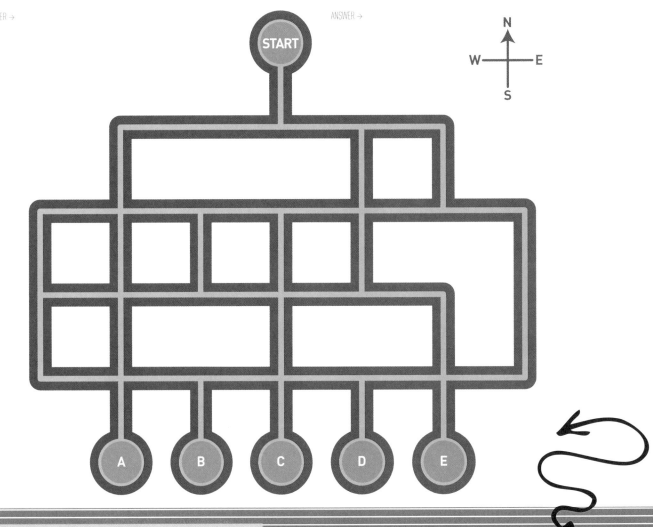

BRIDGE MAZE

ANSWERS PAGE 147

BE WARNED: THIS IS NO ORDINARY MAZE! This marvelous maze includes bridges you must travel under or over as you navigate your way through.

   The very start of the maze is already solved, to show you how it works. See how the path can travel under or over a bridge? Find your way through from the entrance at the top to the exit at the bottom.

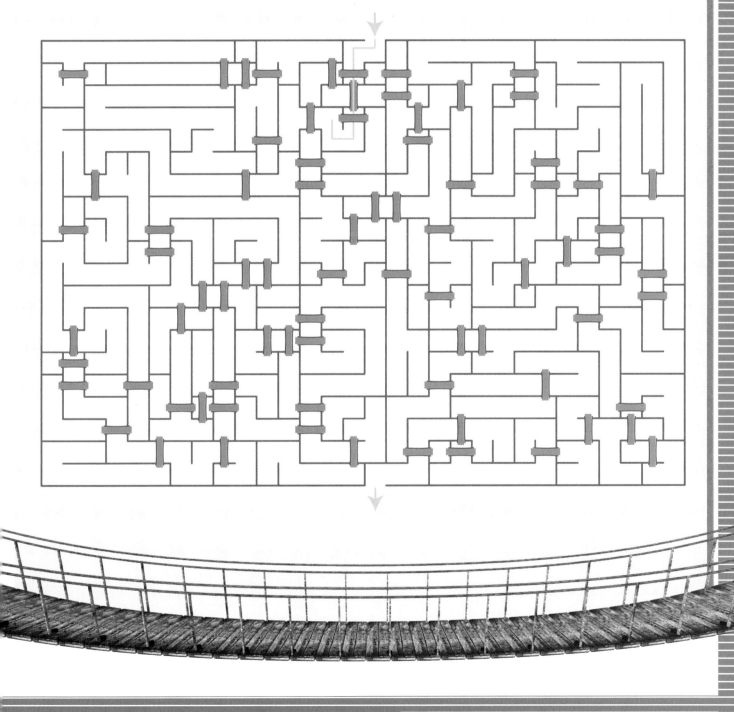

COUNTING SHAPES ANSWERS PAGE 147

EACH OF THESE PICTURES CONCEALS MORE SHAPES THAN IT MAY SEEM TO AT FIRST GLANCE. This picture appears to have nine rectangles, but there are more "hidden" rectangles that can be found by combining two or more rectangles together into a larger rectangle. For example, the large rectangle all around the outside of the picture is one more.

How many rectangles can you find in total?

ANSWER →

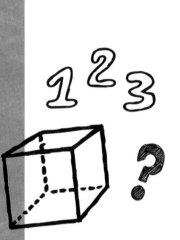

How many triangles can you find in this picture? Remember to look for the "hidden" triangles!

ANSWER →

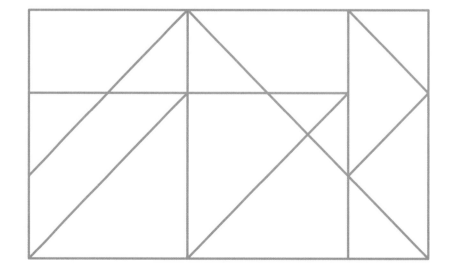

OVERLAPPING PICTURES

ANSWERS PAGE 147

IT CAN BE PRETTY HARD TO MAKE SENSE OF A PICTURE WHEN IT IS OVERLAPPED WITH ANOTHER ONE, because your brain can't be sure whether any particular line or shape is part of one or multiple images. How many dolphins can you count in the picture below? (Hint: They can be different sizes!)

ANSWER →

ODD CUBE OUT
ANSWERS PAGE 147

All of the pictures in each set show the same cube, except for one, which shows a different cube. Which one of each of the sets of cubes is the odd one out?

ANSWER →

ANSWER →

ANSWER →

ANSWER →

MATCHING CUBES ANSWERS PAGE 147

Imagine folding up each of the shapes on the left to make a six-sided cube.
Which one of the four cubes on the right would result in each case?

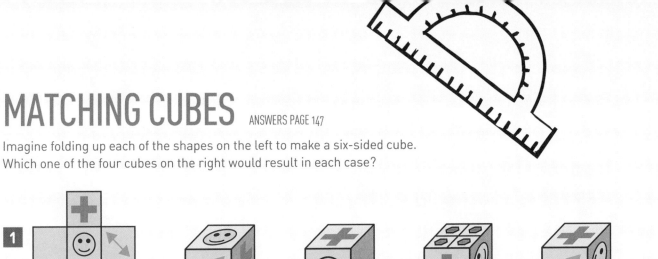

1

A   B   C   D

ANSWER →

2

A   B   C   D

ANSWER →

3

A   B   C   D

ANSWER →

4

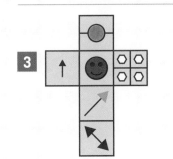

A   B   C   D

ANSWER →

DIRECT DIRECTIONS
ANSWERS PAGE 147

HOW WELL CAN YOU FOLLOW DIRECTIONS? If you follow them correctly, you will reveal a simple picture.

Pick up a pen and draw as described here.

1. Place your pen on the yellow dot.
2. Draw 6 dots right.
3. Draw 1 dot left.
4. Draw 5 dots up.
5. Draw 4 dots left.
6. Draw 5 dots down.
7. Draw 1 dot up.
8. Draw 4 dots right.

YOUR FINISHED DRAWING SHOULD BE A TOP HAT!

RELATIVE DIRECTIONS

ANSWERS PAGE 148

IF YOU ARE GIVEN DIRECTIONS IN THE REAL WORLD, they will usually be relative to which way you would be facing as you traveled along a path or road. See if you can follow these directions to reveal another simple picture. Cross them off as you use them, so you don't lose track of how far down the list you've gone. If you get confused, try placing a small toy on the grid and following the directions with the toy. Point it in the directions shown, and move it as described. This makes it much easier to stay on course!

Can you complete the drawing? Start at the yellow dot, facing in the direction shown by the arrow. Then:

1. Draw five dots forward. Because you are facing the left side of the page, this means you should draw a line across the bottom of the picture.

2. Now turn 90 degrees to the right. You were facing the left side of the page before, so after turning you should now be facing the top of the page.

3. Draw three dots forward. Because you were facing up from the bottom-left dot, this means you should now draw a line joining the bottom-left dot to the dot three dots above it.

4. Now turn 90 degrees right again. This means you are now facing to the right.

5. Draw two dots forward.

6. Turn 90 degrees to the left.

7. Draw one dot forward.

8. Turn 90 degrees to the left.

9. Draw one dot forward.

10. Turn 90 degrees to the right.

11. Draw two dots forward.

12. Turn 90 degrees to the right.

13. Draw two dots forward.

Done!

IF YOU MANAGED TO FOLLOW THE LIST OF INSTRUCTIONS, YOU SHOULD HAVE ENDED UP WITH A PICTURE OF A SIMPLE ROBOT!

JIGSAW PIECES

ANSWERS PAGE 148

CAN YOU COMPLETE THIS JIGSAW PUZZLE without being able to pick up the pieces and try them out? To make it even trickier, some of the pieces are from a different set and so won't fit into the picture.

Circle the four out of seven pieces that will fit into the gaps to complete the puzzle.

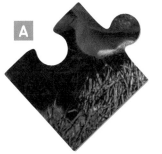

A

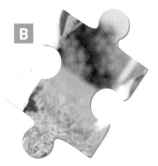

B

C

D

E

G

F

NUMBER LINK

ANSWERS PAGE 148

IN THIS GRID, EACH PAIR OF NUMBERS IS LINKED by a path that travels horizontally and vertically through the grid squares. None of the paths overlap, and only one path goes through each square.

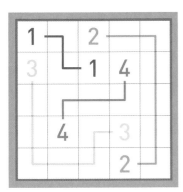

Can you draw a similar set of paths in each of the grids, so that each pair of numbers is linked and none of the paths overlap?

1

	1	2	3	
	4			
1		5		
				3
4	5			2

2

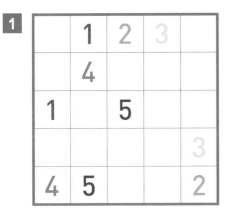

3

CIRCUIT BOARD

ANSWERS PAGE 148

A PIECE IS MISSING FROM THE CENTER OF THIS ELECTRONIC CIRCUIT BOARD. Can you figure out which piece will fit into the gap so that the lines all connect?

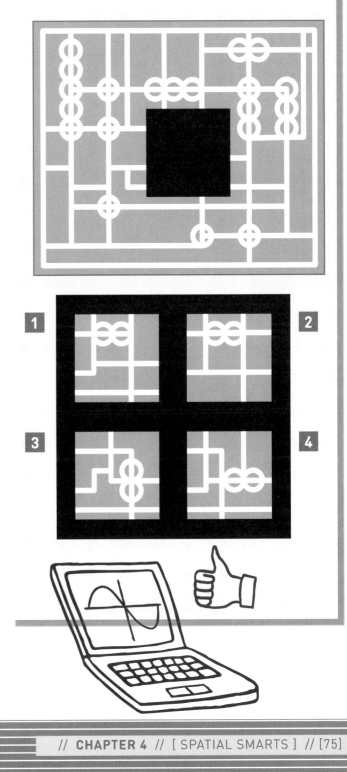

learn

WORD FIT ANSWERS PAGE 148

Place all of the words into the grid, one letter per box, so that every word can be found reading either across or down within the puzzle.

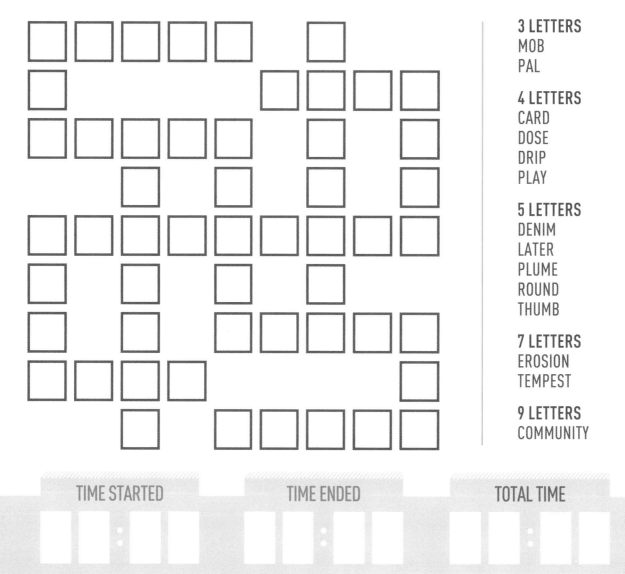

3 LETTERS
MOB
PAL

4 LETTERS
CARD
DOSE
DRIP
PLAY

5 LETTERS
DENIM
LATER
PLUME
ROUND
THUMB

7 LETTERS
EROSION
TEMPEST

9 LETTERS
COMMUNITY

TIME STARTED

TIME ENDED

TOTAL TIME

BUILDING FENCES ANSWERS PAGE 148

Join all of the dots to draw a line that travels through every dot continuously and makes one single loop. To get you started, some dots have already been joined. You can use only horizontal and vertical lines to join dots, and the loop can't cross over itself or use any dot more than once.

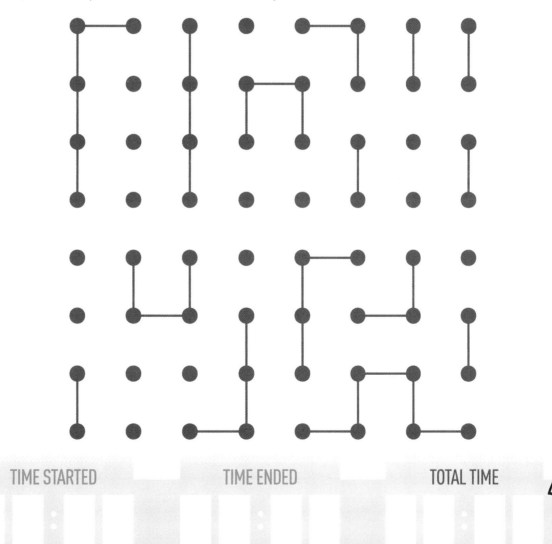

TIME STARTED   TIME ENDED   TOTAL TIME

CHAPTER FIVE

PROBLEM-SOLVING

GROWTH

Above your eyes, right behind your forehead, lies the most important part of your brain. This area, called the frontal lobe, is larger and more developed in humans than it is in any other animal on Earth.

You use your frontal lobe almost every moment of the day. It's in charge of moving your muscles to get you out of bed in the morning, deciding what you eat for breakfast, and figuring out the right answers on your geography test. It steers your emotions, creates your personality, holds your memories, and makes you speak. Because it controls every problem you solve, the frontal lobe is often called the CEO of the brain.

$\rightarrow$

connect learn

ROTATIONAL **PICTURE**

ANSWERS PAGE 148

SOME OBJECTS LOOK EXACTLY THE SAME WHEN THEY ARE ROTATED THROUGH HALF A REVOLUTION (180 DEGREES). Each of the shapes in the picture below is like that: If you were to rotate any of them half a revolution around their centers, marked with the dots, then they would still look the same. It's easy to see this for the squares and rectangles, but a bit trickier for the more complex shapes! Color in each shape to match the color of its dot. The result will be a simple picture of a flower.

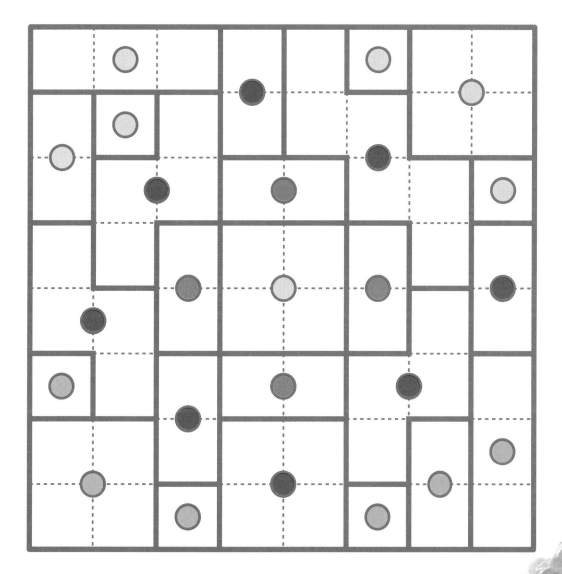

HOW DO WE MAKE DECISIONS?

EVERY DAY, WE FACE THOUSANDS OF CHOICES. SOME OF THEM—LIKE WHETHER TO SNAG THAT SECOND COOKIE—WE MAKE WITHOUT REALLY THINKING ABOUT IT. OTHERS—LIKE WHICH AFTER-SCHOOL SPORT TO SIGN UP FOR—ARE QUESTIONS WE CONSIDER MORE CAREFULLY.

How does your brain make a choice? Recent research shows that your brain's decision-making machinery is complex. The brain uses two different thought networks in two different regions of the brain. One is your valuation network, which constantly sends you information about rewards. You use it when you're trying to decide whether to start studying for your geography test (which won't be fun in the short-term but will reward you with a good grade in the future) or stay on the couch for one more episode of your favorite show (which will reward you with feelings of happiness right now).

To keep you from always choosing short-term rewards—and living on a diet of cookies and cartoons!—your brain has another network, called cognitive control. It helps you work toward big-picture goals. When you shut off the TV and sit down at your desk to study, you can thank your cognitive control network for making the right decision.

TRUSTING YOUR GUT

Some decisions inspire us to make a long list of pros and cons. But for others, we just get a feeling about the path we should choose. We might feel the anxious sensation that a person isn't being honest with us or a tingle that tells us our team is going to win. Can these gut feelings be trusted?

Research suggests they can—and that our intuition can be powerful. In

IF **BABIES' BODIES** GREW AT THE SAME RATE AS THEIR BRAINS, THEY WOULD WEIGH **170 POUNDS** (77 KG) BY **ONE MONTH** OF AGE.

one case, a race car driver had the strong urge to brake as he entered a hairpin turn—but he didn't know why. Even though he knew it could cost him the race, he followed his instinct and slammed on the brakes. As a result, he avoided hitting a pileup of cars hidden around the curve. Trusting his gut saved his life.

But the race car driver didn't know why he'd gotten the urge to brake until he watched a video of the race. He realized that the crowd, which would normally have been cheering him on, was instead staring up ahead at the accident. Though he didn't realize it at the time, his brain unconsciously picked up on the signal. His gut feeling to brake was his brain's way of telling him it had detected that something was wrong. Scientists think sometimes trusting your gut can be a good idea!

YOUR BRAIN: A WORK IN PROGRESS

Teenagers are known for not always making great decisions. They're likely to take risks and make choices they'll later regret. Scientists think their brains are to blame: While the rest of the brain is done developing when we reach adolescence, the decision-making frontal cortex isn't done developing until humans reach their mid-20s.

But the teenage brain doesn't grow more as we reach adulthood. In fact, the opposite happens: As our brains mature, we lose connections between neurons. Between the ages of 13 and 18, our brains grow one percent smaller every year. This might sound like a bad idea, but it works just like pruning a tree: Cutting weaker branches helps the strong ones grow stronger. As we become adults, our brains grow smaller as they get more efficient.

MATH MACHINES ANSWERS PAGE 148

HERE ARE TWO MATH MACHINES! They are easy to operate—just start with the number at the top of the machine and apply each instruction in turn, following the arrows like you would with a flow chart. What number results from each machine?

HINT: Follow the down arrows first.

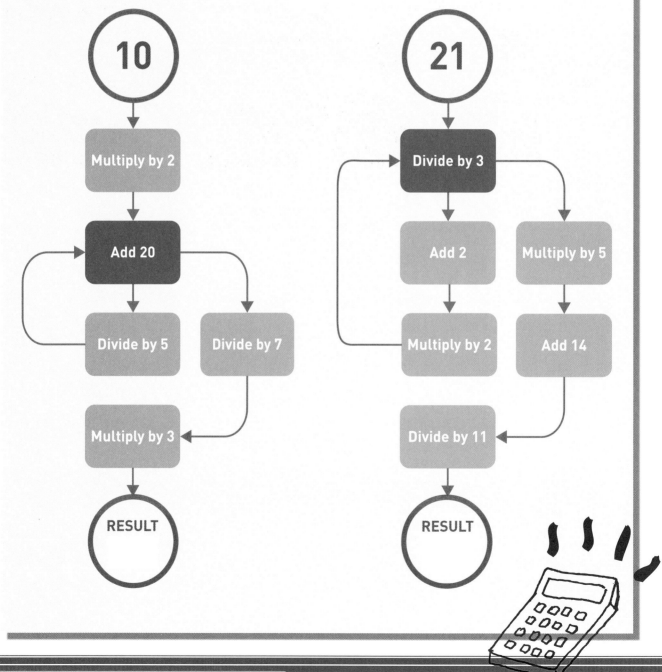

MATH MATCHING ANSWERS PAGE 148

HERE ARE SEVERAL MATHEMATICAL CALCULATIONS. Can you draw lines to join pairs of calculations that have the same result? Each calculation will be part of just one pair, and all calculations will be in a pair. For example, you could join 2+4 to 2×3, since both calculations have the same result: 2+4=6 and 2×3=6.

3×3

4×5

$36 \div 3$

9×5

$10 + 10$

7×4

$19 - 16$

$60 - 15$

$6 \div 2$

$19 - 10$

$21 + 7$

6×2

ROMAN NUMERAL MATH ANSWERS PAGE 148

OUR NUMBER SYSTEM USES 10 DIGITS—0, 1, 2, 3, 4, 5, 6, 7, 8, AND 9—WHICH WE COMBINE TO WRITE ANY NUMBER WE LIKE. The Romans used a different system, based on letters, in which certain letters have a value:

I = 1 **V = 5** **X = 10** **L = 50** **C = 100** **D = 500** **M = 1,000**

To write other numbers, you combine letters and/or repeat letters multiple times. For example, to make the number 3, you would write **III,** or the letter for **1** three times. For the number 20, you would write **XX,** which is the number **10** two times. The letters can be used in any mix, but the letters must always be written from highest to lowest from left to right—so 23 is XXIII, not IIIXX. Here are some more examples of Roman numerals:

II = 2 **VIII = 8** **XI = 11** **XXI = 21** **LX = 60**

Now let's see if you can master some math with Roman numerals. Can you solve these equations, writing your answers in Roman numerals?

$II + III =$ $VI + V =$ $X + LI =$ $X + L + V + C =$

ROMAN NUMERALS

Roman numerals can require a lot of letters to write some relatively small numbers. For example, **9** is **VIIII** (which is the letter for the number **5** plus the letter for the number **1** four times). That's more letters than the word "nine"! So the Romans came up with a shortcut: If you write a single smaller number just before a bigger number, it counts as a **subtraction** from the bigger number. This means you instead write 9 as **IX.** It then means "X minus I," or in other words, 10 minus 1. In the same way, **IV** means "V minus I," or 5 minus 1, which is 4. You can combine these letters for larger numbers, too; to write 59, you would write **LIX,** which is the number 50 (L) plus the number 10 (X) minus 1 (I). Can you imagine trying to do your math homework using Roman numerals?!

DOMINOES

Dominoes is a game played with rectangular "domino" tiles, each with a line dividing its "face" into two squares. Each square has a certain number of spots or is blank. A traditional set has 28 dominoes, with combinations of spots numbering between zero and six, like this:

DOMINO CHAIN

ANSWERS PAGE 148

CAN YOU COMPLETE THIS DOMINO CHAIN BY PLACING THE LOOSE BLUE DOMINOES ON TOP OF THE BLANK WHITE DOMINOES? You can rotate each blue domino as needed. When placed correctly, each touching pair of dominoes should have the same number of dots on the sides where they touch. One blue domino is placed for you, to show how it works. Notice how its four-dotted side is next to another four-dotted side, and its five-dotted side is next to another five-dotted side.

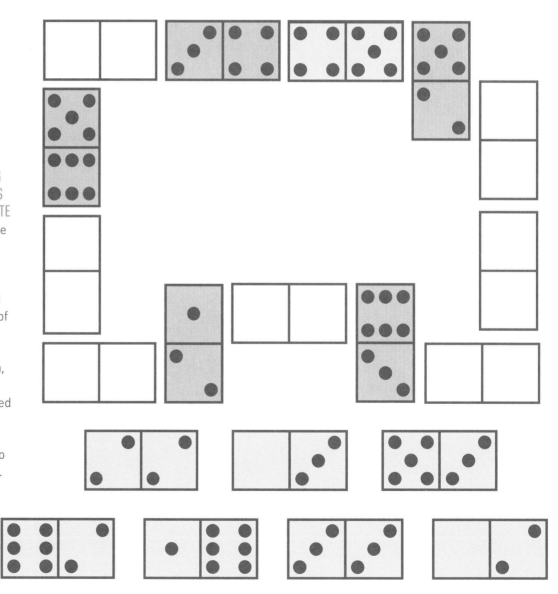

DOMINO PLACEMENT

ANSWERS PAGE 148

INSTEAD OF DOTS, THE DOMINOES IN THIS PUZZLE HAVE NUMBERS ON THEM TO MAKE IT SIMPLER. Can you draw along some of the dotted lines to divide this grid up into a full set of dominoes? Each domino will be used once, so use the check-off chart to keep track of which dominoes have already been placed. Some dominoes have already been marked in the grid to get you started, and they have also been checked off on the chart to show you how it works.

DOMINO MATH

ANSWERS PAGE 149

EACH SIDE OF A DOMINO CAN HAVE A VALUE FROM 0 TO 6, REPRESENTED EITHER BY A BLANK OR A NUMBER OF DOTS. The sides look like this:

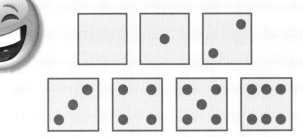

In the old dominoes below, some of the dots have rubbed off. See if you can answer the questions about each of these old dominoes. Empty circles show where dots could be, but only the black dots are actually present on the dominoes.

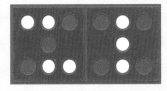

On this red domino, what possible values could the left side have? Three dots are shown, so a "3" is one option for this side of the domino. But what other value could it have?

ANSWER →

What possible values could the right side have?

ANSWER →

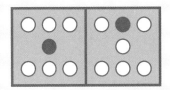

Before some of the dots faded, what possible values could this blue domino have had? Can you list all the different possibilities?

ANSWER →

CARD PROBABILITY

ANSWERS PAGE 149

HAVE YOU EVER PLAYED A GAME OF LUCK, like rolling dice or picking up a hidden playing card? And if so, did you ever wonder how likely you were to get a particular result? Luckily, it turns out that it's not too hard to figure this out: All you need to do is take the number of ways you can get a result and divide it by all of the possible results. So the chance of a "1" on a die is 1 in 6, because there is a single "1" and there are 6 sides.

A normal pack of playing cards has 52 cards, made up of four suits: clubs, diamonds, hearts, and spades. Each suit has 13 cards in it: Ace, 2, 3, 4, 5, 6, 7, 8, 9, 10, Jack, Queen, and King. Diamonds and hearts are red; clubs and spades are black. Write out the probability or give the answer as a fraction.

If you deal one card from a pack of 52 cards, what is the chance that it is red?

ANSWER →

If you deal one card from a pack of 52 cards, what is the chance that it is a 7?

ANSWER →

If you deal two cards from a pack of 52 cards, what is the chance that they are both the same suit?

ANSWER →

CARD LOGIC

ANSWERS PAGE 149

YOU HAVE FOUR PLAYING CARDS, AS SHOWN BELOW: a 4 of diamonds, a 5 of spades, a 6 of hearts, and a 7 of clubs. Can you place them into the 2x2 grid shown in such a way that:
- There is one card per square
- In both columns, the top card has a higher value than the bottom card
- A club is diagonally opposite a diamond
- There is a spade in the bottom row
- There is at least one red card in the right-hand column

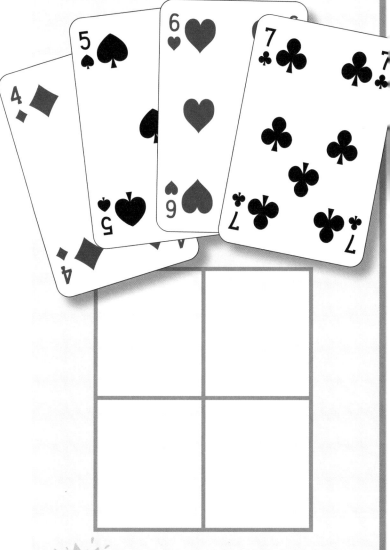

REMEMBER! Columns go from top to bottom and rows go from side to side.

DICE SIDES ANSWERS PAGE 149

IN SOME GAMES YOU ROLL DICE TO FIGURE OUT HOW MANY SPACES YOU SHOULD MOVE. Most dice have six sides, so the results are a random number from one to six. This introduces an element of chance into the game, so it's different each time you play.

But did you know that after rolling a die you can always figure out the number on the underneath of the die without looking? It's easy! Just start with seven and then subtract the number you can see on top. The result will be the number on the bottom. Try it with a real die, if you have one handy—it always works! Put another way, this means that the number on the bottom of the die and the number on the top of the dice always add up to seven.

Using your knowledge of dice, what is the total of the numbers on the underneath of these dice?

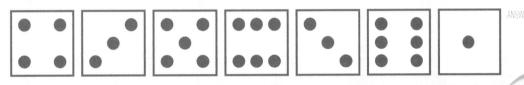

ANSWER →

DICE MATH ANSWERS PAGE 149

A DIE IS USED TO CHOOSE A RANDOM NUMBER. So if you roll a six-sided die, you have a 1 in 6 chance of rolling a one, a 1 in 6 chance of rolling a two, a 1 in 6 chance of rolling a three, and so on. See if you can answer these questions about the chances of rolling different numbers:

What is the chance of rolling a 5 on a die?

ANSWER →

What is the chance of rolling either a 2 or a 3 on a die?

ANSWER →

What is the chance of rolling a number greater than 2 on a die?

ANSWER →

What is the chance of rolling the same number twice in a row?

ANSWER →

CIRCLE LINK ANSWERS PAGE 149

CAN YOU DRAW HORIZONTAL AND VERTICAL LINES TO LINK THESE CIRCLES INTO PAIRS? Each pair should have one blue circle and one red circle, and the lines can't be diagonal or cross either another line or another circle. Here's an example solved puzzle to show how it works:

Now try these two puzzles:

like

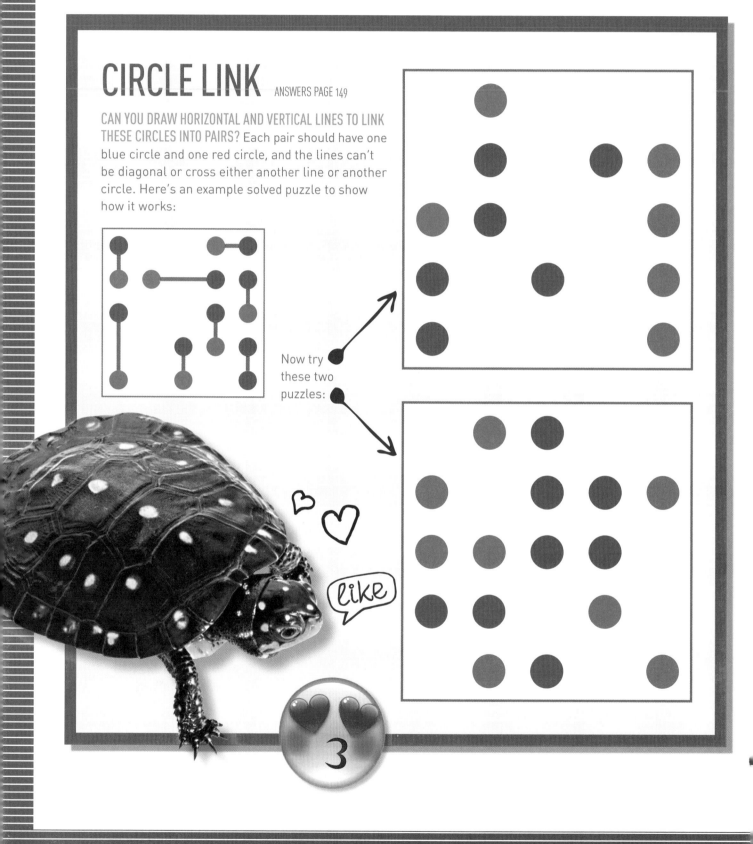

BRIDGES ANSWERS PAGE 149

CAN YOU DRAW HORIZONTAL AND VERTICAL LINES TO JOIN THESE NUMBERED CIRCLES? Each circle should have as many lines connected to it as shown by its number. So, for example, a 3 circle should have three lines connected to it. Lines can't cross over either each other or over another circle and cannot be diagonal. Here's an example solved puzzle to show how it works:

Now try these two puzzles:

SUDOKU ANSWERS PAGE 149

TO SOLVE A SUDOKU PUZZLE, YOU WRITE ONE NUMBER IN EACH EMPTY SQUARE. The goal is to place the numbers in such a way that no number repeats in a row, column, or larger bold-lined box.

Sudoku 4×4: Can you fill the empty squares so that the numbers 1 to 4 appear once in each row, column, and bold-lined 2×2 box?

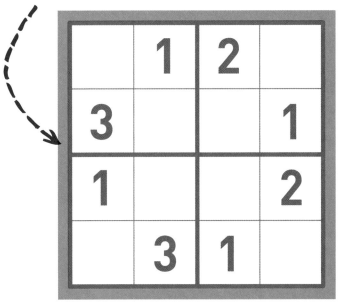

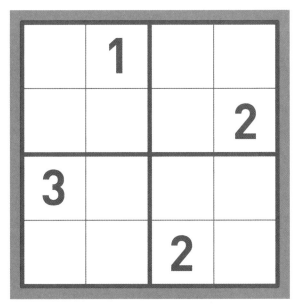

Sudoku 6×6: Can you fill the empty squares so that the numbers 1 to 6 appear once in each row, column, and bold-lined 3×2 box?

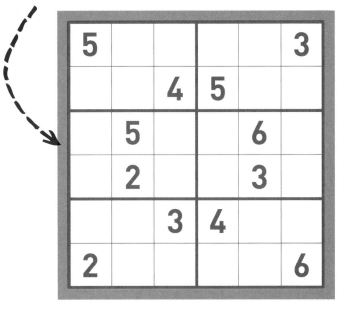

ODD & EVEN SUDOKU

ANSWERS PAGE 150

NOW THAT YOU'VE MASTERED REGULAR SUDOKU, YOU'RE READY TO TRY A VARIATION THAT ADDS AN EXTRA RULE. In this puzzle, **shaded** squares must contain an even number (2, 4, 6 ...), while **unshaded** squares must contain odd numbers (1, 3, 5 ...). As before, numbers cannot repeat within any row, column, or bold-lined box.

PLACE 1 TO 4

PLACE 1 TO 6

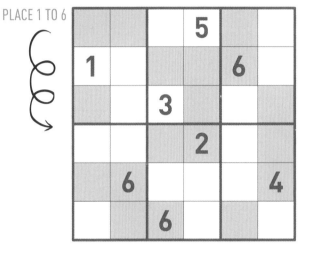

MINDSWEEPER

ANSWERS PAGE 150

MINES HAVE BEEN HIDDEN IN SOME OF THE BLANK SQUARES IN THIS GRID. Numbers tell you how many mines there are in touching squares, including diagonally touching squares. For example, a 3 means that exactly three touching squares contain a mine—no more and no less. Mines cannot be hidden in squares that contain a number, and there can be no more than one mine in any square.

Can you find all the mines in each of these two puzzles?

Here's an example of a solved puzzle so you can see how the numbers relate to the touching mines:

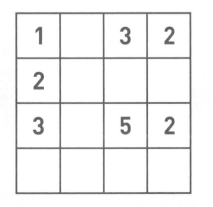

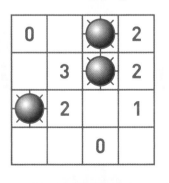

EASY AS A, B, C   ANSWERS PAGE 150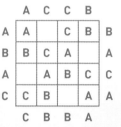

CAN YOU PLACE THE LETTERS A, B, AND C ONCE EACH INTO EVERY ROW AND COLUMN OF THESE 4×4 GRIDS?
Because there are only three letters to place, this means that one square will remain empty in each row and column.

Each letter outside the grid tells you which letter is **nearest** to that letter in the same row or column (either right next to it, or one square away if the nearest square is blank). For example, a "C" above a column means that a C is the first letter in that column, while a "B" at the right-hand end of a row means that a B is the last letter in that row.

Take a look at this example of a solved puzzle to see how it works:

Now try these puzzles, which are arranged in order of increasing difficulty:

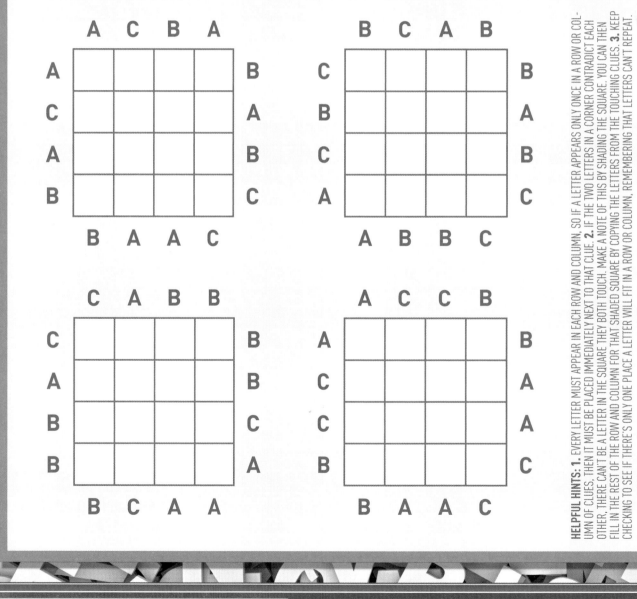

TOUCHY LETTERS

ANSWERS PAGE 150

IN THESE PUZZLES, THE GOAL IS TO WRITE A LETTER IN EACH EMPTY SQUARE SO THAT NO LETTER REPEATS IN ANY ROW OR COLUMN. To make things even trickier, two identical letters cannot touch—not even diagonally. So, for example, you could not have an A diagonally next to another A.

Touchy 5×5:
Use A to E

	E		A	
A	D		E	C
D	B		C	A
	A		B	

	B	E	C	
	C		D	
	D	B	E	

Touchy 6×6:
Use A to F

	E			A	
D					B
		E	B		
		A	F		
A					D
	B			F	

	E			C	
B	C			E	F
F	B			D	E
	A			F	

COLOR BY MATH ANSWERS PAGE 150

TO COMPLETE THIS PUZZLE, YOU'LL NEED TO GRAB YOUR CRAYONS OR YOUR FAVORITE COLORED PENCILS. It doesn't matter if you don't have the exact colors shown here; the hidden picture you will reveal will still make sense if you swap some of them for different colors.

In a typical color-by-number puzzle, you would use a color key to figure out which number goes with which color and then shade every area with the same number in it the same color. This color-by-number puzzle works the same way, except that here you need to flex your math muscles to figure out which color each region should be!

Some shapes are already shaded brown or have no number inside; don't color those in. For all the other shapes, here are the coloring rules:

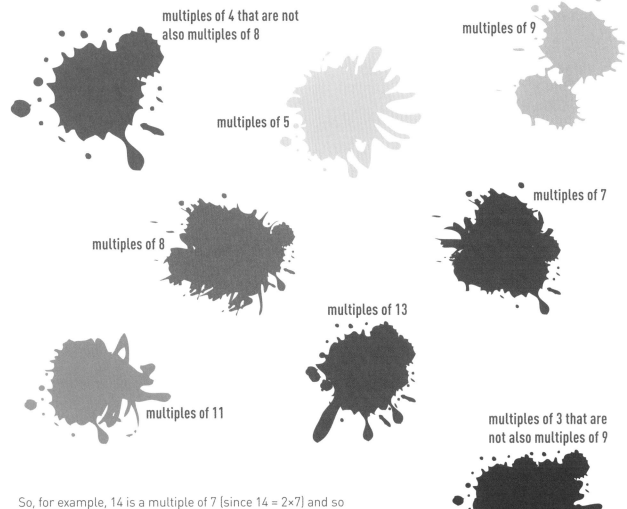

multiples of 4 that are not also multiples of 8

multiples of 9

multiples of 5

multiples of 8

multiples of 7

multiples of 13

multiples of 11

multiples of 3 that are not also multiples of 9

So, for example, 14 is a multiple of 7 (since 14 = 2×7) and so should be colored red. Similarly, 18 is a multiple of 9 (since 18 = 2×9) and so should be colored light blue. As another example, 8 is a multiple of 8 (since 8 = 1×8) and so should be colored green.

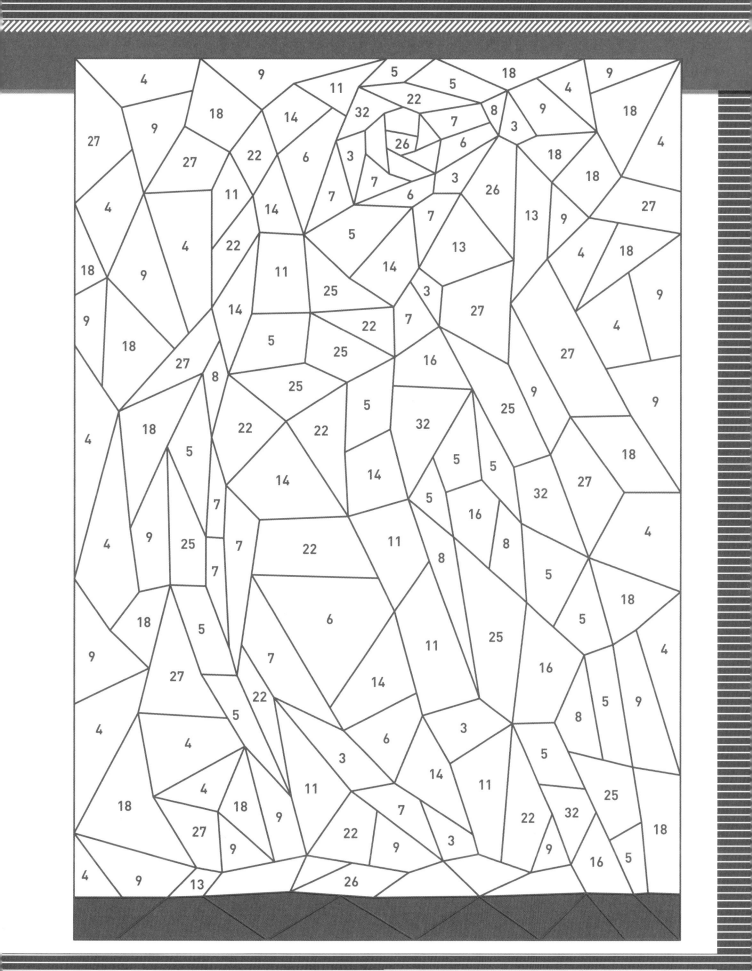

DOT-TO-DOT X3 ANSWERS PAGE 150

IN A NORMAL DOT-TO-DOT PUZZLE, YOU START AT 1 AND DRAW A LINE TO 2, THEN 3, THEN 4, AND SO ON, joining all the dots in increasing numerical order. This puzzle works in the same way, except that you are joining multiples of 3. So you start at 3, draw a line from 3 to 6, then a line from 6 to 9, then a line from 9 to 12, and so on. At each stage you add 3 to the number you are on and then draw a straight line to that next number. Keep going until you have visited every dot! What aquatic animal do you end up with?

HELLO!

Something is fishy here...

DON'T LIFT YOUR PEN

ANSWERS PAGE 150

WHICH OF THESE TWO PICTURES CAN YOU TRACE without lifting your pen from the paper or drawing over a line you have already drawn? You can start with your pen wherever you like.

DID YOU KNOW?

There is an easy way to figure out which pictures can be traced without lifting a pen, no matter how complex the picture. Just count how many lines meet at each point. For the pictures above, each point has either an **even** number of lines meeting at it, shown in white, or an **odd** number of lines (shown in tan). And here's the general rule:

- If there are **no odd points** or **two odd points,** then you **can** trace the image
- For **any other number of odd points** (like the image on the left, which has four odd points), you **cannot** trace the image

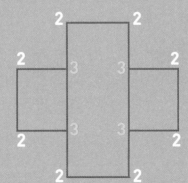
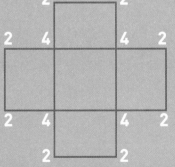

WORD FIT ANSWERS PAGE 151

Place all of the words into the grid, one letter per box, so that every word can be found reading either across or down within the puzzle.

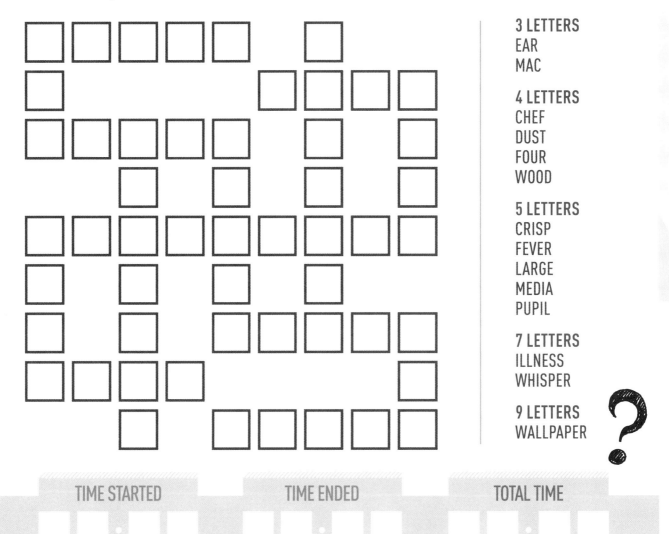

3 LETTERS
EAR
MAC

4 LETTERS
CHEF
DUST
FOUR
WOOD

5 LETTERS
CRISP
FEVER
LARGE
MEDIA
PUPIL

7 LETTERS
ILLNESS
WHISPER

9 LETTERS
WALLPAPER

TIME STARTED

TIME ENDED

TOTAL TIME

BUILDING FENCES ANSWERS PAGE 151

Join all of the dots to draw a line that travels through every dot continuously and makes one single loop. To get you started, some dots have already been joined. You can use only horizontal and vertical lines to join dots, and the loop can't cross over itself or use any dot more than once.

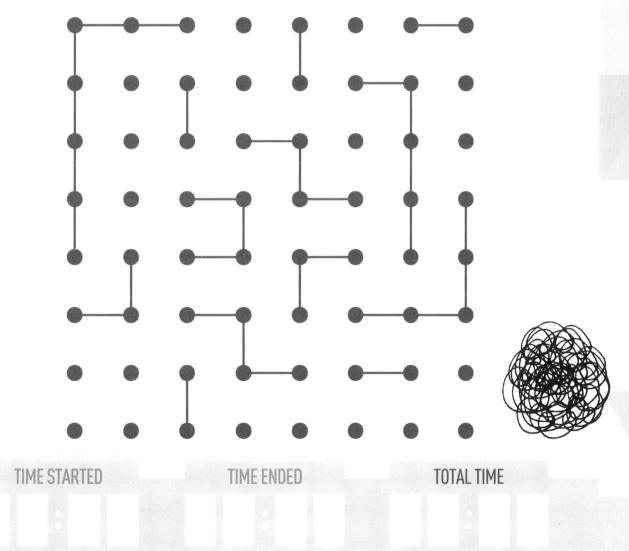

TIME STARTED   TIME ENDED   TOTAL TIME

CHAPTER SIX
MEMORY

Consider some of your most vivid memories. Perhaps you're recalling a trip you took, the first time you rode a two-wheeler, or the day you took home the trophy. Most of us have memories of the important events in our lives. Our memories hold all our past experiences. They shape our relationships and our decisions. Our memories are a big part of who we are.

But what if your most vivid memory didn't happen the way you think? Scientists now know that our memories aren't as trustworthy as they seem. In fact, much of the time, the way we remember things isn't really the way they happened at all.

$\rightarrow$

CAN YOU **RECALL?**

HAVE YOU READ THE TEXT ON THE OPPOSITE PAGE? You'll need to before you answer the following questions. Come back here once you're done!

Let's see how much you can remember of what you've just read:

1) Are our memories always trustworthy?

   ANSWER →

2) When giving examples of memories, what vehicle was mentioned?

   ANSWER →

3) Can you also remember either of the two other example memories that were included?

   ANSWER →

How did you do?

Chances are that you could remember the answer to Question 1, because it came from the paragraph you read more recently. Or maybe the idea just caught your interest, which in itself would also make it more memorable. But you probably found it harder to remember the three examples from the first paragraph, unless you had read the text really slowly and stopped to think of how each of these could apply directly to you.

   If it's tricky to remember details of things you've just read, it's no wonder that your memory is rarely perfect. Just imagine how much less you would remember of the text by this time tomorrow, let alone in a week or two!

MAKING MEMORIES

DO YOU REMEMBER WHAT YOU WERE DOING WHEN YOUR FAVORITE TEAM WON THE CHAMPIONSHIP GAME? SCIENTISTS KNOW THAT MANY PEOPLE FORM "FLASHBULB" MEMORIES OF WHERE THEY WERE AND WHAT THEY WERE DOING WHEN SOMETHING HUGE AND UNEXPECTED HAPPENED.

EYEWITNESS EVENTS

In 1978, a psychologist named Elizabeth Loftus conducted a now famous study. She showed college students a series of photographs depicting a car accident in which a red sedan knocks down a pedestrian. Then she asked the students questions about what had happened. Some of the questions were misleading, such as "Did another car pass the red sedan while it was stopped at the yield sign?" when the photographs showed it was actually a stop sign. When the researchers later quizzed the students about what happened during the accident, those who had been given misleading questions were more likely to give incorrect answers. The experiment showed that memories aren't a reliable record of a past event. Instead, they can be changed by new information learned after the event occurred.

Flashbulb memories are especially unreliable. Someone might recall that when their team won they were wearing a red jersey and eating popcorn. But when these memories are later tested, most of the details they remember so vividly turn out to be wrong. Now some scientists think they might know why.

MOST PEOPLE CAN **HOLD ABOUT SEVEN DIGITS** IN THEIR HEAD FOR ABOUT **30 SECONDS.**

A GAME OF TELEPHONE

It might seem like our memories work like filing cabinets—we jot down an experience, file it away, and then pull it out and review it every time we recall the event. But experiments have hinted that, instead, memory is more like a game of telephone within your brain: Every time you recall a memory, you change some details. The more often you pull up the memory, the further it gets from the truth.

This explains why people's flashbulb memories of momentous events are especially untrustworthy—we think and talk about these memories so many times that they become extra distorted.

MOST PEOPLE **CAN'T RECALL** MEMORIES FROM BEFORE THEY WERE **3 OR 4** YEARS OLD.

THE PEOPLE WHO CAN'T FORGET

Ask Jill Price to recall every Easter since 1980 and she can tell you the date, the grade she was in, who she celebrated with, and what the weather was. In fact, Price can remember every day of her life since the age of 12! She's one of the few people in the world with a "highly superior autobiographical memory" (HSAM for short).

This condition is a mystery to science: Brain scans show that the memory centers of people with HSAM—the hippocampus and prefrontal cortex—are no different than the average person's. Instead, experts think the key might lie in their thinking patterns. Studies have shown that people with HSAM are extremely sensitive to the details around them: the smells, colors, and feelings of an event. That might help them create stronger memories—recalling, for example, the day of the week and the weather on July 10, 2005—while the rest of us can barely remember what we ate for breakfast.

PICTURES OF PEOPLE

START BY COVERING THE BOTTOM HALF OF THIS PAGE. You'll see why in a moment! Next, take a look at the following eight people. Spend as long as you like trying to learn the name of each person.

Once you're ready, move the covering to the top half of the page so that you can now see only the bottom half—and keep reading below.

AIDEN   MING   EMMA   LIAM

OLIVIA   LUCAS   SAMIRA   ASHA

Here are the same eight people. Can you write the correct name of each person beneath their picture?

If you get stuck, the names of the people are written at the bottom of this page. Does having the names help?

AIDEN, ASHA, EMMA, LIAM, LUCAS, MING, OLIVIA, SAMIRA

MATCHING PEOPLE

ANSWERS PAGE 151

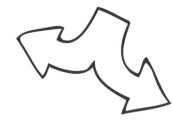

START BY COVERING THE BOTTOM HALF OF THIS PAGE. Now spend a minute or two looking at the 20 photographs of people at the top of this page. Make sure you look at each face in turn, so that you might be able to recognize these people if you saw them again. Once you're ready, cover the top half of the page instead so that you can now see the bottom half—and keep reading below.

Here are 20 people. Some of them you have seen already, and some of them are different. Can you put a check mark under the photographs that you saw on the top half of the page?

[BEHIND THE BRAIN]

Did you notice that there were 20 faces on this page but only eight faces on the previous page? And yet ... didn't you find it at least a little bit easier to remember which faces you'd seen, rather than the names of the people you'd seen? This is because your brain is really good at remembering pictures—and especially faces—that it's seen before. If you've ever taken some photos and then later looked through a mix of yours and other people's photos, it's usually really easy to remember which ones you took, even if it's been a long time since you snapped the original photograph.

You'll probably always find it harder to remember the name of someone than to remember that you've seen their face—which is not surprising, because to remember a name you have to first of all remember that you've met them in the first place, so it's a more complex task. A good way to remember someone's name is to try to connect it with their appearance, especially in a silly way. For example, if someone has long hair and their name is Lily, you could think "long-haired Lily," which might just be silly enough that next time you will remember their name along with their face!

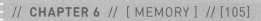

NAMES AND POSITIONS

IT'S NOT JUST PEOPLE'S NAMES THAT CAN BE HARD TO REMEMBER: Names of places can be tricky to recall, too. If a place has some meaning to you, you probably have little trouble remembering its name. But places that you've never been to are much harder to learn. This is especially true if you don't know anything much about them, which is one reason why there are very few people who can name every country in the world!

Let's try remembering the names of some state capitals. First, look at this list. Spend a minute or so trying to remember them and the order they're in.

OKLAHOMA CITY	MONTGOMERY
HONOLULU	BOISE
AUGUSTA	HARTFORD
SPRINGFIELD	JACKSON
AUSTIN	SALEM

Once you're ready, cover them up and try to list them below.

How did you do? You probably didn't remember them all—if you did, then you have done incredibly well—so take a look at the bottom of the page for the full list of names. Now that you have seen the names again, can you remember where the remaining cities fit in the table?

AUGUSTA, AUSTIN, BOISE, HARTFORD, HONOLULU, JACKSON, MONTGOMERY, OKLAHOMA CITY, SALEM, SPRINGFIELD

SOME INITIAL HELP

IT'S MUCH HARDER TO REMEMBER 10 SEPARATE STATE CAPITALS THAN JUST ONE OR TWO.
So wouldn't it be great if you could convert a list of 10 places into a much smaller list of items to remember? Well, you can—kind of. The secret is to create a compact "memory aid" for the places you want to remember. The memory aid can then be used as a trigger to help you remember all of the places.

Let's see how this can work. Start by looking at the first column below (the purple one). Read down that column and look at the initial letters, highlighted in bold. They spell out "SMALL." Now all you need to do is remember the word "SMALL" (this is your memory aid) and you have made it much easier to remember both the cities and the order they are in. It isn't a perfect memory aid, since you still need to remember which city goes with which letter, but it does make it a lot easier!

The green column is a bit trickier, since the first letters don't happen to spell out a word. No problem! You just need to come up with your own memory aid. The first letters are "PJDAD," which you could maybe remember as two words: "PJ" and "DAD" ... maybe by thinking of a father in pajamas? Or perhaps a father in banana-patterned pajamas—the sillier an image is to you, the easier it is to remember.

Now read the list of cities again, and take note of which city is associated with each letter of "SMALL" and "PJ DAD." Once you're ready, cover the top half of the page and try to list them on the bottom half of the page.

SPRINGFIELD	**P**HOENIX
MADISON	**J**UNEAU
ATLANTA	**D**ENVER
LANSING	**A**LBANY
LINCOLN	**D**OVER

Can you fill in this table so that it contains the same state capitals in the same positions?

Did you do better this time? Was it simpler with the two memory aids, SMALL and PJ DAD, to prompt your memory?

If you don't remember all of the names, then take a look at the list at the bottom of the page. Can you complete the table now?

ALBANY, ATLANTA, DENVER, DOVER, JUNEAU, LANSING, LINCOLN, MADISON, PHOENIX, SPRINGFIELD

GRID RECALL

ANSWERS PAGE 151

HOW GOOD IS YOUR VISUAL MEMORY? At the top of this page are four squares, each of a different color. Within each square, some of the squares are shaded and some are not.

Can you copy these shaded grid squares onto the larger, empty grid beneath? The green square to the right should be copied onto the green area below, the yellow square onto the yellow area, and so on. But there's a twist! You need to do the copying from memory.

Start by memorizing the green square. Then, once you're ready, cover it with a small piece of paper so you can't see it. Next, redraw it on the larger square beneath, purely from memory. Once you're done, uncover it and see if you were correct. Finally, repeat those steps with the other three squares. A simple picture will result.

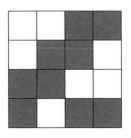

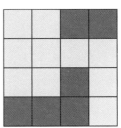

WINNER

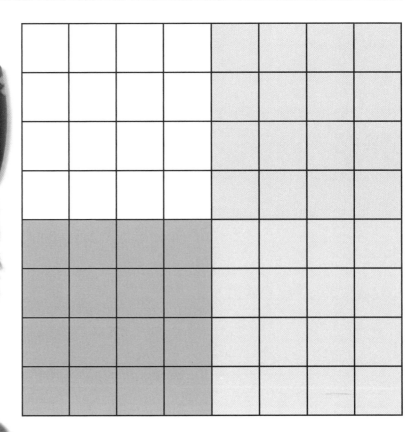

DOT CONNECTIONS

ANSWERS PAGE 151

HERE'S ANOTHER MEMORY TEST, broken into seven separate parts that get trickier to remember as you go along!

Start with the brown area at the top left. It is a 3×2 grid with three black lines drawn on it. Study the brown grid until you are sure you have memorized it, then cover it with a small piece of paper and draw it as accurately as you can on the brown area on the large, empty grid below.

Then repeat with the six other grids, one by one, covering each one before copying it from memory. You'll end up with a simple picture when you're done.

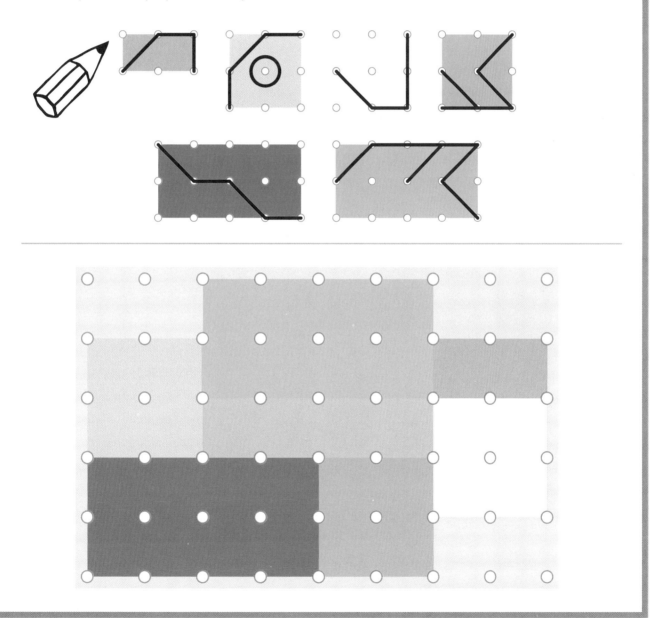

SORTED SHAPES

LOOK AT SET ONE BELOW, which consists of four shapes, and remember what order they're in: The square is first, the triangle is second, and so on.

Once you've learned the order, cover them up and look down to Recall One below. These are the same shapes, but in a different order. Can you write a number from 1 to 4 beneath each shape to put them in the order they were originally? So you would write "1" beneath the square, "2" beneath the triangle, and so on.

Next, once you've tried the first set with four shapes, try doing the same with the second set of seven shapes. Finally, try the third set with nine shapes!

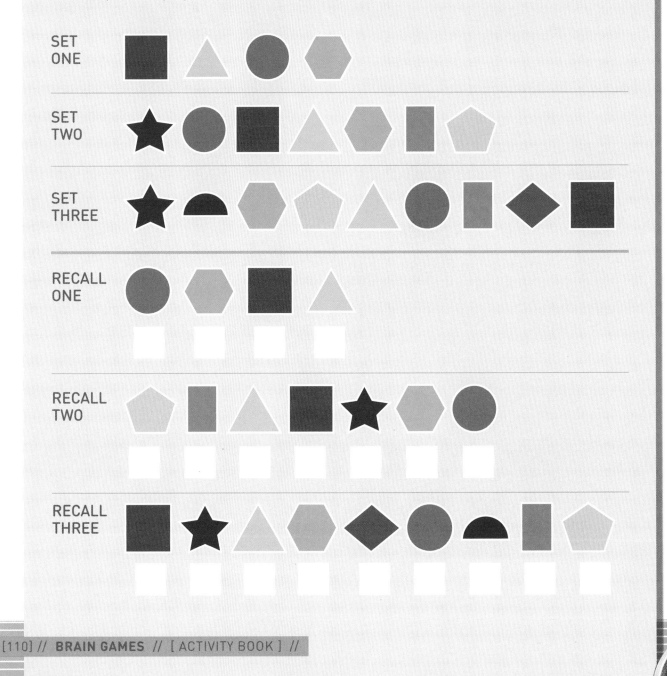

MEMORY PALACES

ONE POWERFUL SECRET WAY TO REMEMBER THINGS IS TO CONNECT THEM TO YOUR HOUSE OR TO A FAMILIAR BUILDING—somewhere you know really well and can imagine walking through. The key is to come up with a fixed route through the rooms in the building and use it every time you want to either learn or recall something. For example, you might enter into a hall, then pass into a living room, go on to a kitchen, and then into a utility room (or whatever makes sense for you). It's important that it's familiar to you, so you don't have trouble remembering the route itself.

Now say you are heading to the store and you have four items you need to remember: milk, bread, lettuce, and juice. You "put" one item in each room as you follow the imaginary route through the building. But—and this is really important—you need to try and put the objects in ridiculous places, because funny or amusing things are much easier to remember! So you might have milk pouring down the walls of the hall and then, in the living room, pass a table built out of bread. Next up, in the kitchen, you see lettuce sprouting out of the faucet, and then, in the laundry room, the washing machine is full of juice cartons.

What four objects did we just place in our imaginary house? You can recall them back by walking through the house on the fixed route and "seeing" what's in each room. For example, you start in the hall; what's weird about the hall? Well, obviously it's the milk running down the walls! Using this method, you can remember a set of items with much less effort. It also works if you need to remember what order they are in. Your house is called a "memory palace" because you place all the precious things you want to remember there.

VISIT YOUR PALACE

Now try it out by learning this shopping list of **four items.** You can use the palace described above until you have a chance to build your own. The journey is: hall, living room, kitchen, and laundry room.

Test yourself later to see if you can still remember these items. (We'll also ask you if you can still remember them in a couple of pages.) If you need to, make a note of "hall, living room, kitchen, laundry room," unless you have already created and used your own memory palace.

Apples
Ice cream
Potatoes
Pizza

BUILDING YOUR PALACE

Love

But what if you want to remember more things than you have rooms?

No problem: You just need to invent extra rooms! Why not put a swimming pool in the basement and a game room next to your bedroom? Another way to add rooms to your memory palace is to combine multiple real locations. How about a mishmash of your home and your school? Or your house and a friend's place? It might take you a bit of effort to learn your extended memory palace, but once you've learned it, you'll be able to use it forever—and it will make any future lists much easier to remember.

SUBSTITUTIONS ANSWERS PAGE 151

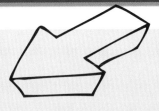

Cover the bottom half of this page and take a good look at the objects in the picture directly below this paragraph. Try to remember what's there and then, once you're done, cover the top half of the page instead.

Now it's time to test your memory! Which of the items in the picture below were *not* in the top picture? Circle them.

Did you spot the new objects? Now can you also remember which items from the top picture are missing from the bottom one? You might find this trickier! Write the names of the missing objects here:

ANSWER →

ADDITIONS

ANSWERS PAGE 151

Cover the right side of this page and study the following pieces of fruit. Try to remember what's there and how much there is of it.

When you're ready, cover the left side of the page and reveal the right side instead.

Some extra pieces of fruit have been added. Circle them.

Did you spot all of the extra fruit? If you're not sure, then try the memory test in reverse: Cover the right side of the page and then see if you can figure out what's missing on the left half! Write your answer here:

ANSWER →

COLOR RECALL

ANSWERS PAGE 151

START BY FINDING A SET OF COLORED PENS OR PENCILS. You'll need light blue, blue, yellow, orange, red, green, and brown. Next, remember the order that these colors are in and assign a number for each color based on its order in the list:

COLOR KEY

1 = LIGHT BLUE	**3 = YELLOW**	**5 = RED**	**7 = BROWN**
2 = BLUE	**4 = ORANGE**	**6 = GREEN**	

Then, once you think you'll remember this list, cover it up and read the bottom part of the page.

Now it's time to use your colored pens or pencils! In the picture to the right, color each shape labeled "1" with the color that came first in the list, color the "2"s with the color that came second, and so on for all seven colors. As you go, you'll reveal a hidden picture using the power of your memory!

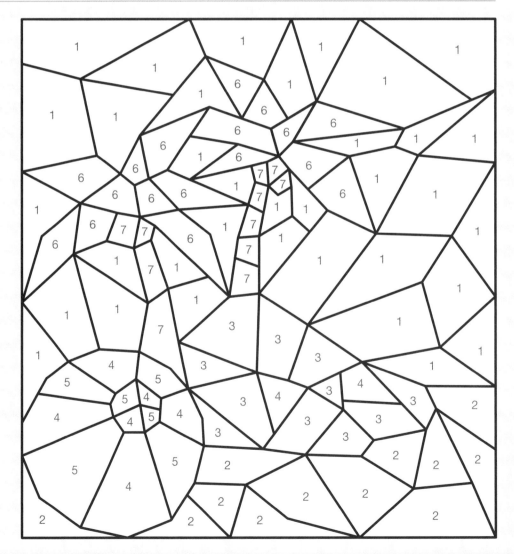

DOTTY TEST ANSWERS PAGE 151

HOW GOOD ARE YOU AT REMEMBERING NUMBERS? For this puzzle, you need to learn three number ranges (meaning six numbers in total):

| 1 – 22 | 34 – 42 | 50 – 58 |

If you have trouble remembering them, experiment with ways of making them meaningful—for example, the first could be remembered as one 1 and then two 2s (to make 22). Once you're ready, cover the top of the page and continue below.

In the picture to the left, draw a series of straight lines to join the first number of each pair to the second number of each pair—but you must travel via all of the in-between numbers. So, for example, if a line went from 5 to 8, then you would join 5 to 6, 6 to 7, and 7 to 8. Repeat for all three pairs to reveal a hidden picture (but don't join any other numbers!).

REMEMBERING NUMBERS

HOW DID YOU DO IN THE PREVIOUS PUZZLE? Remembering numbers can be surprisingly tricky! Even so, everyone does need to remember numbers from time to time, whether it's an emergency phone number, the date of an event, or even somebody's age.

To make learning numbers easier, it can help to group them in some way. The way we "group" the digits in a telephone number, for example, is actually a great example of how this works. Let's say you need to remember a phone number:

(205) 555-1012

In this number, the "groups" are **205, 555,** and **1012.** Instead of remembering the phone number as **2, 0, 5, 5, 5, 5, 1, 0, 1,** and **2**—as 10 separate digits—the way it's written encourages you to remember it as fewer, larger numbers.

Grouping digits together in this way is called **chunking.** The basic idea is to reduce the number of things you need to remember by making each item slightly more complex. With a little practice, you can remember much longer numbers than you would otherwise be able to.

TRY IT YOURSELF

See if you can use a chunking technique to remember each of the following numbers. Experiment with splitting them up in different ways. Look at each number for as long as you like, then cover it up and see if you can write it out successfully below.

5050	11/1/19
202122	(205) 555-8989

ANSWER →

BONUS!
REMEMBER THE MEMORY PALACE TECHNIQUE FROM A COUPLE OF PAGES AGO? IF SO, CAN YOU USE IT TO REMEMBER THE FOUR GROCERY ITEMS YOU WERE ASKED TO LEARN AT THE END OF THE PAGE? WRITE THEM HERE IF YOU CAN:

ANSWER →

MEMORY MATH

ANSWERS PAGE 151

YOU CAN PROBABLY REMEMBER A SMALL NUMBER OF ITEMS very briefly without having to try to learn them. This ability taps your "short-term" memory, and it's why you can read this sequence of digits **1 3 8 4** ... and then, so long as you do it shortly afterward, recite them back without trouble. You don't instantly forget them. But you probably will within 30 seconds—unless you've made some conscious effort to actively remember them (by reading them several times, for example).

You can generally remember between five and seven items in your short-term memory, which is one reason why mental arithmetic can be tricky: It's natural to start forgetting numbers as you calculate them, unless you practice paying attention to them!

TRY THE FOLLOWING MEMORY GAME TO SEE HOW YOU DO.

For each of the following sets of two or three numbers, look at them for no more than a few seconds and then cover them and answer the question immediately next to them (which you should not read in advance).

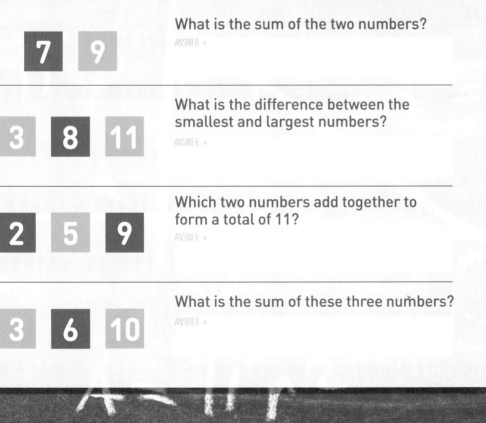

7 **9**		**What is the sum of the two numbers?** ANSWER →

What is the difference between the smallest and largest numbers?
ANSWER →

3 **8** **11**

Which two numbers add together to form a total of 11?
ANSWER →

2 **5** **9**

What is the sum of these three numbers?
ANSWER →

3 **6** **10**

WHAT IS PROCEDURAL MEMORY?

INFORMATION THAT YOU WANT TO REMEMBER BEYOND THE NEXT FEW SECONDS needs to be stored in your "long-term memory." When you have to recall it some time in the future, you rack your brain and try and recollect these facts—with varying degrees of success!

But did you know there are some memories that you can always recall without any effort? And that they actually become harder to recall when you think about them too much? You may be surprised to learn that some of these memories are essential to your everyday life.

UNCONSCIOUS MEMORIES

When you were a baby, you learned to walk—and every early step involved a real effort that could lead to you falling flat on the floor. But now that you're older, you walk without even thinking about it.

GIVE IT A TRY: How hard is it to explain the process of walking? You don't know precisely what you do with your legs and feet and arms as you walk; your body remembers everything you learned about how to walk. This is an example of a procedural memory—when the body learns how to do a certain "procedure" and then applies it without conscious effort.

LEARNING NEW PROCEDURES

YOU CAN PICK UP A PEN AND WRITE YOUR NAME, BUT—like most people—you're probably able to do this with only one hand: the hand you usually write with, known as your dominant hand. If you try with the other hand—your nondominant hand—you will probably find it surprisingly hard. You might even discover that you suddenly are unable to remember how to write some letters!

Though most people will always write better with one hand than the other, you can still improve your ability to write with the other hand (or even with your feet, amazingly!). Try this out for yourself by taking a notepad or some scrap paper and spending a few

minutes writing a couple of sentences with your nondominant hand. Unless you are ambidextrous (able to use both hands equally well), it might not look great—but that doesn't matter.

Try doing this again tomorrow. Then try again the day after tomorrow, and the day after that, and so on for a week or more, if you want. Keep writing in the same notepad, or keep the bits of scrap paper so you can compare them. After a little practice, you will start to get better and find that it requires less conscious effort. This is an example of learning a new procedural memory.

LEARNING TO JUGGLE

MANY TASKS THAT SEEM COMPLEX CAN ACTUALLY BE LEARNED SURPRISINGLY QUICKLY, thanks to the power of your brain's procedural memory. If you've ever tried to juggle, you might have decided that you would never be able to do it. But if you practice for 15 minutes a day for just a week or two, you might suddenly surprise yourself with your new abilities!

TRY IT FOR YOURSELF

Find three balls that are small enough to hold comfortably in your hand and aren't too light or so heavy that it takes a lot of effort to throw them a few feet into the air. Be sure to go to a place where you won't knock anything over!

Start with one ball in your dominant hand and practice throwing it upward in an arc so that it lands in your other hand. And then try throwing it back to your dominant hand. Keep practicing for a bit until this starts to get easier. It might take a few days before you can throw the ball up into the air and back and forth between hands without regularly dropping it, but letting your brain learn is key to learning to juggle.

Once you feel confident, start with two balls in your dominant hand and one in your nondominant hand. It's time to juggle three balls! Throw one of the balls from your dominant hand to your other hand, but before it lands in that hand, throw the ball from that hand back toward your dominant hand. And then, before that lands in your hand, you should throw the remaining ball up in the air toward the other hand. Try to also catch as many of the three balls as you can.

Performing those three moves will take a lot of concentration, and you might not catch all (or any) of them for a while. But practice for a few days and your brain will start to develop that procedural memory.

BEHIND THE BRAIN

Procedural memory allows you to learn physical tasks that don't require too much mental effort. While you perform these tasks, you can use your body almost automatically while focusing your mind on other things.

Learning to play the piano is a great example. When you first sit at a piano, the sea of white and black keys can be intimidatingly vast. But, after a few lessons, you start to become familiar with the sensation of resting your fingers on the keys and playing some notes. It starts to take less conscious effort to press a key, and you can begin to concentrate (just a bit!) on actually making music.

Over time, your brain learns more and more about the act of physically playing the piano, and you no longer need to consciously think about the speed and pressure that each of your fingers is exerting.

You can learn to play simple tunes on the piano pretty quickly, but if you wanted to be a professional pianist you would have to spend thousands of hours practicing. But those hours need to be spread over many days. If you were to spend 10 hours a day for 100 days, you would learn nowhere near as much as spending an hour a day for 1,000 days. Your brain needs time to learn from your practice, which it does while you sleep. In fact, sleeping and resting well are really important for learning procedural memories. So next time you need to learn a physical task, aim for frequent, relatively short sessions rather than a few really long sessions.

WORD FIT ANSWERS PAGE 151

Place all of the words into the grid, one letter per box, so that every word can be found reading either across or down within the puzzle.

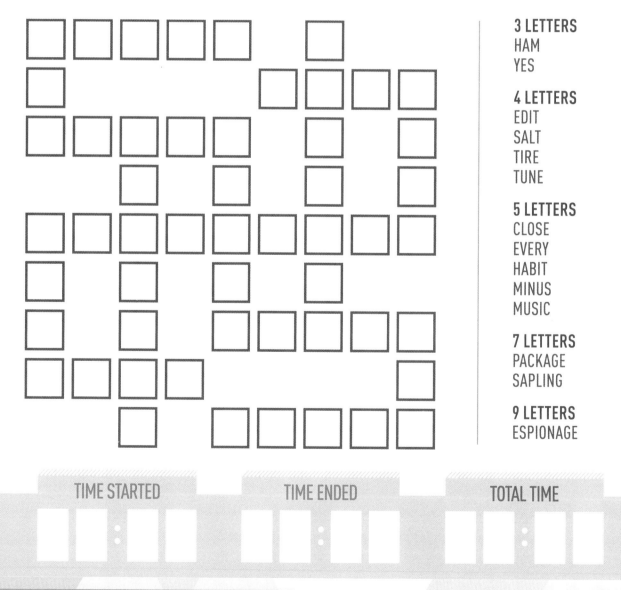

3 LETTERS
HAM
YES

4 LETTERS
EDIT
SALT
TIRE
TUNE

5 LETTERS
CLOSE
EVERY
HABIT
MINUS
MUSIC

7 LETTERS
PACKAGE
SAPLING

9 LETTERS
ESPIONAGE

TIME STARTED

TIME ENDED

TOTAL TIME

BUILDING FENCES ANSWERS PAGE 152

Join all of the dots to draw a line that travels through every dot continuously and makes one single loop. To get you started, some dots have already been joined. You can use only horizontal and vertical lines to join dots, and the loop can't cross over itself or use any dot more than once.

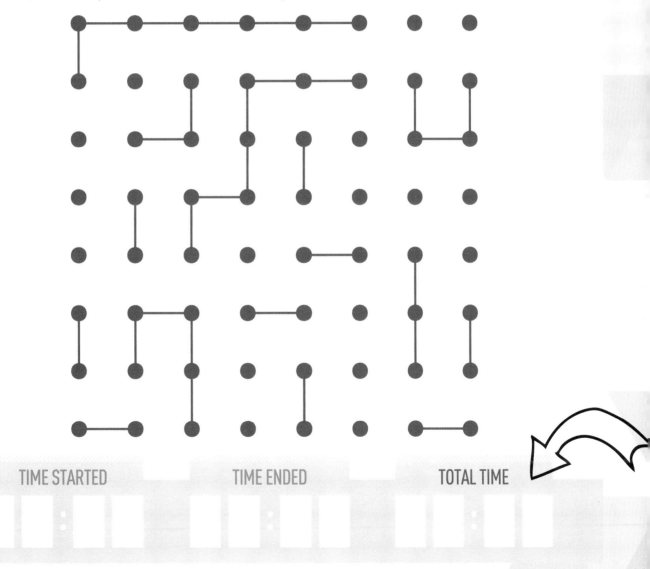

TIME STARTED   TIME ENDED   TOTAL TIME

CHAPTER SEVEN

BRAIN MYSTERIES

Why do we dream? How do we store our memories? And what exactly are emotions?

Brain scientists can use scanning technology to watch the brain in action. They can watch blood flow through the brain and observe as electrical activity lights up different regions. They've mapped each area of the brain and know what it does.

But despite everything they've learned about how the brain works, they've just begun to scratch the surface. After all, the human brain is the most complex object in the universe. Brain scientists say we're only beginning to understand about how that three-pound (1.4-kg), gray-pink lump of flesh makes us who we are.

$\rightarrow$

IT MUST BE **OBVIOUS**

ANSWERS PAGE 152

IF SOMEONE TOOK A PHOTO OF A DINOSAUR WANDERING THROUGH THE HALLS OF YOUR SCHOOL, YOU'D THINK IT WOULD BE PRETTY OBVIOUS IN THE PICTURE, WOULDN'T YOU? You might be surprised at your ability to notice it, actually! When an object or animal is moving, it's usually pretty easy to see. But when it stays still, it can blend in with its surroundings and be *much* harder to spot! That's especially true in the picture below, in which the dinosaurs are surrounded by lots of people who obscure your view of them. See if you can spot the four hidden dinos in this picture:

WHAT IS REALITY?

LOOK AROUND YOU. WHATEVER YOU CAN SEE—YOUR BEDROOM, A SCHOOL BUS, A PARK—IS IT ALL REALLY THERE?

As we live our daily lives, we tend to think that the sights, sounds, and smells that we perceive are showing us the real world. But ... it's not true! If you don't believe it, consider how optical illusions can fool our brains into seeing something that isn't there. And think about how brain conditions like synesthesia—which might cause someone to not only hear a song but also taste each note—show us that one person's reality is not *everyone's* reality.

That involves a surprising amount of guesswork. For example, only 10 percent of the information your brain uses to construct what you see comes from your eyes; the other 90 percent comes from various parts of your brain. That means our brains are not just experiencing the world through our senses, like a person watching a film. They're actually *creating* our perception of the world all the time—more like an artist painting a picture.

BEING A BRAIN

Imagine being a brain. You're closed up inside a skull, and it's your job to figure out what's going on outside. There's no light or sound in there. All you have to work with is a flood of electrical impulses shooting in from all the senses at once. It's up to your brain to reconstruct these signals into a picture of the outside world.

CHANGING YOUR MIND

Studies have even shown that our perception of the world is flexible. In one experiment, volunteers stood on the 10-yard line of an American football field, faced the goal post, and gave an estimate of the goal post's size. Researchers then instructed the volunteers to try kicking a football through the goal post 10 times. After that, researchers asked the participants to estimate the goal post's size again.

The results were surprising: Poor kickers, who had kicked the ball through the goal post two or fewer times, estimated the goal post to be about 10 percent narrower the second time around. The good

BASEBALL PLAYERS PERCEIVE THE BALL AS **LARGER** WHEN THEY'RE **HITTING WELL** AND **SMALLER** WHEN THEY'RE HITTING **POORLY.**

kickers, who scored three or more times, perceived the goal post as about 10 percent wider than on their first estimate. The experiment suggests that our experiences can affect how we see what's around us.

Reality, it turns out, is just something our brains think up. How they do it is one brain science mystery we're just beginning to unravel.

CAN WE BUILD A BRAIN?

Computers are a modern marvel. Today, we have machines that can search the skies for faraway planets, diagnose diseases, and even beat the best human players at complex games like chess.

In 2015, researchers built the world's first artificial neurons that communicate using electricity, just like the ones in your skull. In 2017, researchers created an artificial synapse (the connection between neurons) that can "learn." These artificial synapses become better at conducting electricity the more they are used—exactly the same way learning works in the brain.

Some experts think that someday we'll be able to use brain-inspired technology like this to power robots that can learn from their mistakes and adapt to our needs. Will an artificial brain have emotions? A personality?

What do you think? Will a brain made of plastic be a machine—or will it be alive?

SOME EXPERTS ESTIMATE THAT IT WOULD TAKE THE **ENERGY** OF AN ENTIRE **POWER PLANT** TO RUN A **COMPUTER** AS SMART AS THE **HUMAN BRAIN.**

SPOT THE COLOR-BY-PIXEL DIFFERENCE ANSWERS PAGE 152

YOU'LL NEED SEVEN COLORED PENS OR PENCILS FOR THIS PUZZLE: red, pink, yellow, blue, light blue, green, and light green. First, color in the picture on this page according to the color key next to it. Then, when you're finished, color in the picture on the opposite page using the (different) key above that picture.

COLOR KEY

1 = LIGHT BLUE

2 = WHITE (LEAVE UNCOLORED)

3 = BLUE

4 = PINK

5 = RED

6 = YELLOW

7 = GREEN

8 = LIGHT GREEN

1	1	1	2	1	1	1	1	1	1	1	1	2	1	1	1	1	1	1	1	1	1	1	1	1	1	1	1	1	1	1
1	1	1	1	1	1	1	1	1	1	1	1	1	1	1	1	1	1	1	1	1	1	3	3	3	3	1	1	1	2	1
2	1	1	1	1	3	3	3	3	3	3	1	1	1	1	1	1	1	3	3	4	4	4	3	3	1	1	1	1	1	1
1	1	1	3	3	3	4	4	4	4	3	3	3	1	1	2	1	3	3	5	5	5	4	4	3	3	1	1	1	1	1
1	1	1	3	4	4	4	5	5	4	4	4	3	3	1	1	3	3	5	5	5	5	5	4	4	3	1	1	1	1	1
1	1	3	3	4	5	5	5	5	5	5	4	4	3	1	3	3	5	5	5	5	4	5	5	4	3	1	1	1	1	1
1	1	3	5	5	5	4	4	4	4	5	5	4	3	3	3	5	4	4	5	5	4	5	5	4	3	1	1	1	1	1
2	1	3	3	5	5	5	5	5	4	5	5	4	4	3	3	5	4	5	5	4	4	5	4	4	3	1	1	1	1	1
1	1	1	3	5	4	5	5	5	5	5	5	4	4	3	5	5	4	5	5	4	5	4	4	3	3	1	1	1	1	1
1	1	2	3	5	4	4	5	5	5	5	5	6	6	6	5	5	5	5	5	4	4	3	3	1	1	1	1	1	1	1
1	1	1	3	3	4	4	4	5	5	6	6	6	6	6	6	6	5	5	4	4	3	3	1	1	1	1	1	1	2	1
1	1	1	1	3	3	3	5	5	5	5	5	6	5	6	5	6	5	6	5	5	3	3	3	1	1	2	1	1	1	1
1	1	1	1	1	1	3	3	3	5	6	6	6	6	5	6	5	6	6	6	3	3	3	3	1	1	1	1	1	1	1
1	2	1	1	1	1	1	1	3	3	6	6	6	5	6	6	5	6	6	6	5	5	3	3	1	1	1	1	1	1	1
1	1	1	1	1	1	1	3	3	3	3	6	6	5	6	5	6	6	6	6	5	4	4	4	5	3	3	3	1	1	1
1	1	1	2	1	3	3	5	5	5	3	6	5	6	5	6	5	6	5	5	5	4	5	5	5	3	1	1	1	1	1
1	1	1	1	3	3	4	5	4	4	5	6	6	6	6	6	6	5	5	5	5	5	5	5	5	3	3	1	1	1	1
1	2	1	1	3	4	5	4	5	5	5	5	5	6	6	7	5	3	5	4	5	5	5	5	5	5	3	1	1	1	1
1	1	1	1	3	4	5	4	4	5	5	4	5	3	7	7	3	3	4	5	5	4	4	5	5	5	3	1	1	1	1
1	1	1	3	4	4	5	4	5	5	4	4	3	8	7	7	8	3	4	4	5	5	4	4	5	5	5	3	1	1	1
1	1	1	3	4	4	5	4	5	4	3	3	8	7	7	7	8	3	4	4	5	5	5	5	5	5	3	1	1	1	1
1	1	1	3	3	4	5	5	5	5	3	3	8	8	7	7	8	8	3	3	4	4	4	4	4	4	3	1	1	1	1
1	1	1	1	3	4	4	4	5	3	3	8	8	8	7	7	8	8	8	3	3	3	3	3	4	4	3	3	1	1	1
2	2	1	1	3	3	3	3	3	3	8	8	8	1	7	7	1	8	8	8	8	1	3	3	3	1	1	1	1	1	1
1	1	1	1	1	1	1	1	8	8	8	8	1	7	7	7	1	1	8	8	8	8	1	1	1	1	1	1	1	1	1
1	1	1	1	1	1	1	8	8	1	1	7	7	1	1	1	1	1	8	8	1	1	1	1	1	1	1	1	1
1	1	1	1	2	1	1	1	1	1	1	7	7	7	1	2	2	1	1	1	1	1	1	1	1	2	1
1	2	1	1	1	1	1	1	1	1	1	7	7	1	1	1	1	1	1	1	1	1	1	1	1	1
1	1	1	1	1	1	1	1	1	1	1	1	7	7	1	1	1	1	1	1	1	1	2	1	1	1	1	1	1

COLOR KEY

1 = BLUE	2 = YELLOW	3 = LIGHT BLUE	4 = PINK
5 = RED	6 = WHITE (LEAVE UNCOLORED)	7 = LIGHT GREEN	8 = GREEN

```
1 1 1 2 1 1 1 1 1 1 1 1 1 2 1 1 1 1 1 1 1 1 1 1 1 1 1 1 1 1 1 1
1 1 1 1 1 1 1 1 1 1 1 1 1 1 1 1 1 1 1 1 1 1 3 3 3 3 1 1 1 2 1
2 1 1 1 1 3 3 3 3 3 3 1 1 1 1 1 1 1 1 3 3 4 4 4 3 3 1 1 1 1
1 1 1 3 3 3 3 5 5 5 5 3 3 3 1 1 1 3 3 4 4 4 5 5 3 3 1 1 1
1 1 1 3 5 5 5 4 4 5 5 5 3 3 1 1 3 3 4 4 4 4 4 5 5 3 1 1 1
1 1 1 3 5 4 4 4 4 4 4 5 5 3 1 3 3 4 4 4 4 5 4 4 5 3 1 1 1
1 1 1 3 4 4 5 5 5 5 4 4 5 3 3 3 4 5 5 4 4 5 4 4 5 3 1 1 1
2 1 1 3 4 4 4 4 4 4 5 4 5 5 3 3 4 5 4 4 5 5 5 3 1 1 1
1 1 1 3 4 5 4 4 4 4 4 4 5 5 3 4 4 5 4 4 5 4 5 5 3 1 1 1
1 1 2 3 4 5 5 4 4 4 4 4 6 6 6 6 4 4 4 4 5 5 3 3 1 1 1 1
1 1 1 3 3 4 5 5 5 4 4 6 6 6 6 6 6 4 4 5 5 3 3 1 1 1 1 2
1 1 1 1 3 3 3 4 4 4 4 6 4 6 4 6 4 6 4 4 3 3 3 1 1 2 1 1 1
1 1 1 1 1 1 3 3 3 4 6 6 6 6 4 6 4 6 6 3 3 3 3 1 1 1 1 1 1
1 2 1 1 1 1 1 1 3 3 6 6 4 6 4 6 4 6 6 4 4 3 3 3 1 1 1 1
1 1 1 1 1 1 3 3 3 6 6 4 6 4 6 6 6 4 4 5 4 4 3 3 1 1 1
1 1 1 2 1 3 3 4 4 4 3 6 4 6 4 6 4 4 4 5 5 4 4 4 3 1 1
1 1 1 1 3 3 5 4 5 5 4 6 6 6 6 6 6 4 4 4 4 4 4 4 3 3 1
1 2 1 1 3 5 5 4 4 4 6 6 7 3 4 5 4 4 4 4 4 4 4 3 1
1 1 1 1 3 5 4 4 5 5 4 4 5 4 3 7 7 3 3 5 4 4 5 4 4 4 3 1
1 1 1 3 5 5 4 4 4 5 5 3 8 7 7 8 3 5 5 4 4 5 5 4 4 3 1
1 1 1 3 5 5 4 4 4 4 5 3 3 8 7 7 8 3 3 5 5 4 4 4 5 3 3 1
1 1 1 3 3 5 5 4 4 4 3 3 8 8 7 7 8 8 3 3 5 5 5 5 5 3 1 1
1 2 1 1 3 5 5 5 4 3 3 8 8 8 7 7 8 8 8 3 3 3 3 5 5 3 3 1 1
1 2 1 1 3 3 3 3 3 3 8 8 8 1 7 7 1 8 8 8 8 1 3 3 3 1 1 1 1
1 1 1 1 1 1 1 1 8 8 8 1 7 7 7 1 1 8 8 8 8 1 1 1 1 1 1
1 1 1 1 1 1 1 1 8 1 1 1 7 7 1 1 1 1 1 8 8 1 1 1 1 1 1
1 1 1 2 1 1 1 1 1 1 1 7 7 1 2 2 1 1 1 1 1 1 1 1 1 2 1
1 2 1 1 1 1 1 1 1 1 7 7 1 1 1 1 1 1 1 1 1 1 1 1 1
1 1 1 1 1 1 1 1 1 1 1 7 7 1 1 1 1 1 1 1 1 1 2 1 1 1 1 1 1
```

Apart from the change in colors, did you also notice that there are eight other differences between the two pictures? If not, can you find them all now? Circle them on the pictures or list them here.

[BEHIND THE BRAIN]

Did you notice the differences before you were asked above? If you didn't, that's not unusual! When you study something really closely, it can be hard to see the "big picture." Because you were looking closely at individual squares in each image, you didn't have the chance to sit back and see if there were any changes between them **other** than the colors. The change in colors also made it harder to easily spot differences, because the color change was so obvious to your eyes that it obscured the other, smaller differences.

WORD HUNT ANSWERS PAGE 152

FOR THIS CHALLENGE, YOU'LL NEED A STOPWATCH SO YOU CAN TIME—IN SECONDS—HOW LONG IT TAKES YOU TO SOLVE EACH PUZZLE. You don't need to be exact, but be as accurate as you can. First, try these puzzles:

#1 List two colors—one that is four letters long and one that is six letters long:

4 LETTERS __ __ __ __

6 LETTERS __ __ __ __ __ __

Your time: _____ seconds

TOTAL TIME FOR
BOTH QUESTIONS: [   ] SECONDS

#2 List three fruits—one that is five letters long, one that is six letters long, and one that is nine letters long:

5 LETTERS __ __ __ __ __

6 LETTERS __ __ __ __ __ __

9 LETTERS __ __ __ __ __ __ __ __ __

Your time: _____ seconds

NOW THAT YOU'VE COMPLETED THE FIRST TWO, let's make it a little trickier! In these puzzles, your solutions must start with a specific letter. Do you think you'll be quicker or slower now that there are fewer possible words to choose from? Try them and find out:

#3 List two colors—one that is three letters long and starts with R and one that is five letters long and starts with G:

3 LETTERS R __ __

5 LETTERS G __ __ __ __

Your time: _____ seconds

TOTAL TIME FOR
BOTH QUESTIONS: [   ] SECONDS

#4 List three fruits—one that is four letters long and starts with P, one that is six letters long and starts with O, and one that is 10 letters long and starts with S:

4 LETTERS   P __ __ __

6 LETTERS   O __ __ __ __ __

10 LETTERS   S __ __ __ __ __ __ __ __ __

Your time: _____ seconds

HOW DID YOU DO? Were you faster on the first two questions or the second two questions? Let's try one more word hunt challenge.

#5 List two colors—one that is three letters long and ends in N and one that is five letters long and ends in E:

3 LETTERS __ __ N

5 LETTERS __ __ __ __ E

Your time: _____ seconds

TOTAL TIME FOR BOTH QUESTIONS: _____ SECONDS

#6 List three fruits—one that is four letters long and ends in E, one that is six letters long and ends in A, and one that is 10 letters long and ends with N:

4 LETTERS __ __ __ E

6 LETTERS __ __ __ __ __ A

10 LETTERS __ __ __ __ __ __ __ __ __ N

Your time: _____ seconds

[BEHIND THE BRAIN]

For many people, questions 3 and 4 would have been the quickest to fill in. Even though being given the first letter of the answers meant fewer possible colors or fruits for you to choose from than in questions 1 and 2, having the first letter of something usually makes it **easier** for us to think of a possible word. Think of it this way: Have you ever felt that a word was on the "tip of your tongue"? This effect is caused by your brain only being able to *half* retrieve a word—it starts to look it up from the first letter, but then gets stuck! It leaves you with that annoying feeling that you can *almost* remember it. This is all down to how our brain works: We fetch words from our memory based on the first letter. Being given the first letter in questions 3 and 4 above skips over the first part of the recall process, making it easier (sometimes!) to think of words that can fit. Conversely, we **don't** retrieve words from our memory based on their **last** letter, so you probably found questions 5 and 6 the hardest of all.

Easy

EASY READING

READ THE FOLLOWING TWO SIGNS—one triangular and one circular:

ROME IN THE THE FALL

What do you think of of the latest blockbuster movie?

Did you spot anything unusual about either of the signs? If not, try reading them again.

If you're still unsure, try counting the number of words in "Rome in the fall"—it's four words here in this text. How many words are there in the triangle?

Now take a look at the circle again. Can you spot something similar that's wrong with that, too?

[BEHIND THE BRAIN]

Each of the signs contains a repeated word, and yet it's incredibly easy not to notice this. Perhaps you **did** notice it, in which case, congratulations! But most people **don't** notice the extra words—even in the triangular sign, where there are far fewer words than on the circular sign.

Why is it so easy **not** to notice the repeated words? Believe it or not, it's because your brain is really clever! When you read, you usually don't need to consciously take note of each individual letter. You can glance at a *p* and *know* it's a *p* without thinking, *There's a loop and a straight line below, so that must be a* p. You learned to identify the letters when you were younger, and now you don't need to think about it anymore (unless someone has *really* bad handwriting!).

Similarly, you don't need to take special note of the words you know well. When you look at a common word like "the" or "of," you pay very little attention to it beyond registering how it connects the rest of the sentence together. For you to understand the meaning of the sentence, there's no real need for you to know that the word has been written twice—so your brain doesn't bother telling you! It skips over the unimportant bits, so you don't need to spend a lot of effort stopping to think about what the repeated word might **mean**—when it really only means that someone made an error (or, in this case, deliberately created a puzzle to trick you!).

LETTER COUNTS

OOPS!

TRY READING THE STRANGE SENTENCES BELOW, counting the number of letter f's as you go:

Farmers frequently fetch faithful French folk fifty farmyard friends. Foxes free ferrets from fields founded for foolish fish.

ANSWER →

HOW MANY LETTER F'S DID YOU COUNT?

That sentence had a lot of f's in it! Try again with this sentence, which has fewer f's:

Far fewer f's makes a sentence easier to read, for if it has foggy passages of fuzzy facts, then for all of the time you study it you are at risk of falling asleep.

ANSWER →

HOW MANY LETTER F'S DID YOU COUNT?

Now take a look at the small text at the bottom of the page and see if you were correct.

[BEHIND THE BRAIN]

The first paragraph has a *lot* of f's in it. But they are mostly easy to count because every word has at least one f, so you naturally concentrate on each word as you go and successfully add it to your count.

The second paragraph, however, is much harder to count because a lot of the words don't have f's, so you need to remember to pay close attention as you go. This means that it's incredibly easy to miss one of the f's in the two "of"s, or even the f in "if." The hardest one of all to count is the f in the "of" in "of falling," because your eye naturally jumps to the next line and gets distracted by the f in "falling."

Why is the second paragraph easier to miscount? It's because words like "of" are so common that you pay little attention to the precise letters on the page—your brain identifies the word for you without any conscious effort and quickly moves on to the next word in the sentence.

The first paragraph has 20 f's. If you got fewer, did you count both of the f's in "faithful" and "fifty"? The second paragraph has 13 f's.

MOVEMENT AND REPETITION

THE PICTURES ON THIS PAGE AND AT THE TOP OF THE OPPOSITE PAGE MAY LOOK COMPLEX, BUT THEY'RE ACTUALLY PRETTY SIMPLE DESIGNS: The one below is a single curve rotated and repeated many times, and the one to the right is a zigzag line repeated many times. You don't have to stare at this circle for long before it starts to "move."

The repeated spiraling curves give the *idea* of movement as you look toward the center of the circle. The lines become thinner the closer they get to the center; because it is difficult for your eyes to focus on them, the result is a shimmering effect as your eyes search around for something they can lock on to.

The many lines in this image look like they are moving, creating a sliding effect as your eyes try to make sense of the image. The horizontal "lines" formed by the corners might even seem to wobble upward and downward as you look across the page.

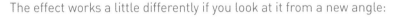

The effect works a little differently if you look at it from a new angle:

Now the stripes appear like steps. It's easier for your brain to make sense of the image when it's rotated this way, although it still appears to shimmer. Also, if you look at it from a slight distance, do you find that the diagonal stripes appear to be two different shades of yellow?

YESSS!!!

[BEHIND THE BRAIN]

When you are looking at something close up, such as when you're reading, your eyes make lots of jerky movements: They stop and look at something, then jump to look at something else, and repeat that continuously. These movements—so small that you aren't aware of them—are why the pictures on these two pages appear to shimmer when you look at them: Your eyes are jumping around, so the movement is coming from your eyes rather than from the page itself. Why does your eye make these small jumping movements? Only the very center of your eye sees the world in a high resolution, so your eye needs to move around to build up the detailed picture you see.

FOLLOWING FACES

TAKE A LOOK AT THIS PHOTOGRAPH. Is the person looking straight at you? Wow—they are!

Now put the book down, prop it up, and look at it from some distance. Is the person still looking at you? What if you move a bit to the side? Or if you move the other way? As you move around, do their eyes follow you?

It's a strange effect, but you can easily re-create the same result. Just take a picture of yourself looking straight at the camera, with the camera directly in front of you and at the same height as your eyes. Then, as you look at the resulting picture of yourself, your eyes will follow you around the room. Freaky!

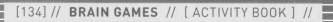

FLOWER POWER

THE MOVEMENT OF REAL FLOWERS IS REMARKABLE, since many flowers open as the sun rises, turn their heads to follow the sun throughout the day, then close again as the sun sets. But did you know that pictures of flowers printed on paper can move, too?

Take a look at the floral illusion below, letting your eyes wander around the page. Does it look like the flower is growing and shrinking in front of your very eyes? Move your eyes in loops around the image and notice how the middle continues to expand while the outer leaves shrink toward the center. You could also try looking at something just to the right of the book and moving your eyes around a little—the sensation of the image moving at the edge of your vision can be a little unsettling!

WHOA!

The paper isn't really moving, of course, so what's happening? The bright white and dark black borders on the petals look like the effect of light and shadow, but they are placed at different angles on different parts of the image. As your eyes move around the image, your brain continually adjusts its impression of the image based on the changing light, making it appear to shift as it reinterprets the rest of the scene.

SHAPE IDENTIFICATION

LOOK AT THIS PICTURE. There are three shapes, all the same. What type of shape are these?

Now that you've identified the shapes above, do the same again with the three shapes below. What type of shape are these?

Did that seem like a very basic test of your ability to recognize shapes? Well, it is—and, depending on the answers you gave, maybe it also *isn't!*

When you look at the top three shapes, do you see diamonds? And when you look at the bottom three shapes, do you see squares?

But wait ... they are actually *identical* shapes, except that the ones at the top of the page have been rotated by 45 degrees. You can measure the shapes with a ruler and a protractor (or anything with a 90-degree corner, like a book or set square) if you want to check!

Even if you answered "square" for both, you can probably still see that the shapes at the top of the page could easily be called diamonds—and the lower shapes are definitely squares.

It's perfectly correct to call each set of shapes either squares or diamonds, so why did your brain come up with one name for one set and a different name for the other? Well, it's because your brain is heavily influenced by the context in which it sees things. In real life, gravity usually ensures that everything sits flat on the floor, so you don't normally need to worry about the unlikely event that a square-shaped object could have been balanced on a point! So you see diamonds at the top and squares at the bottom. Something similar happens with more complex objects and shapes, too, as you'll see on the next page.

CUBE COMPREHENSION

LOOK AT THIS PICTURE. It's a drawing of a 3D object—specifically, it's a picture of a cube, as if you're looking down at it from above.

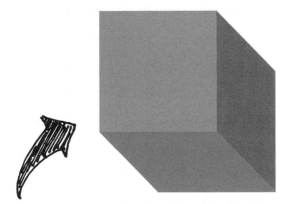

Look at it again. Can you *also* imagine it as a room you are looking into from the front? See if you can picture it both ways!

You can't perceive it as both a cube and a room at the same time, though. By shifting your focus to different parts of the picture, you should be able to make it "pop" back and forth between a cube and a room.

If you're having trouble seeing both versions, this might help:

1. In the cube view, the point where the three colors meet is at the bottom right of the top of the cube, looking down.

2. In the room view, the point where the three colors meet is at the back-right bottom corner of the view into the room.

It's easier to make sense of the picture as a cube when it's drawn this way:

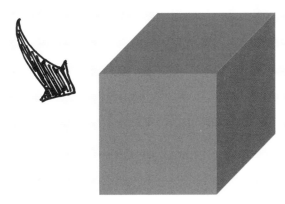

Since you're used to seeing cubes from this point of view—that is, you don't normally stand over a cube and look down on it—this may more immediately look like a cube to you than the first picture did. It's also possible to see this version of the cube as a room. But now your perspective is that the room's corner is in the upper right instead of the lower right, which makes it trickier to see than before.

It's interesting how a mirror image of a picture can look so different! It all has to do with the assumptions your brain makes about the world and what it's likely to be looking at.

If you thought all of that was strange, then can you also see all of the following pictures as cubes, too?

The top picture is the same cube as to the left, but without the colored faces. Even though you can see through it, you probably still have no trouble seeing it as a cube.

In the middle picture, the cube is rotated so you're looking straight on at a corner. Can you still see a cube?

In the bottom picture, you have a similar view as in the middle picture except that your perspective is slightly higher up above the cube. Can you still see it as a 3D object?

Even in the final picture it's still possible to see a cube, even though it's actually just a hexagon with three lines joining opposite corners! It's amazing how your brain can see such a simple drawing and come up with another interpretation for it.

FLOATING IN SPACE

YOUR EYES WORK TOGETHER TO HELP YOU JUDGE HOW FAR AWAY SOMETHING IS FROM YOU. Each of your eyes sees a slightly different image because they are (on average) about 2.4 inches (6 cm) apart. Your brain combines the different images it receives from each eye to form one 3D image.

But as you've already learned from previous puzzles, your brain can sometimes be tricked when it tries to make sense of a flat picture in a book. That's because the flat images in a book lack depth, so it's like looking at the world with only one eye open.

Try closing one eye and pointing your two index fingers at each other, like this:

Now can you move your hands slowly together, still keeping one eye shut, so that your two fingertips touch?

Was it much harder than it looks?

Open both eyes and try again, and it's suddenly much easier. This shows how powerful your sense of depth is ... and why you have two eyes!

Your two eyes usually have a very similar view of the world, so you don't get confused by the small differences between what each eye can see. But if something is so close to your eyes that they see *completely* different images, then it can become a bit confusing. Your brain has to guess at what it's really seeing.

YOU CAN USE THIS EFFECT TO MAKE A "FLOATING" MAGICAL FINGER APPEAR RIGHT IN FRONT OF YOUR EYES. Just place the tips of your fingers pointing at each other as above, close to your eyes. Then stare at something in the distance, and slowly move your fingertips toward each other, so they move across in front of your eyes.

As they move closer, suddenly a magical floating finger appears in midair, like this:

You should be able to see the floating "finger" fairly clearly. Keep your focus in the distance, and start to move both hands slowly away from your face and—remarkably—the floating finger moves away, too! It might even get easier to see. Eventually it does start to shrink, however, and once it's far away enough from your face it will vanish completely.

ARTIFICIAL BRAINS   ANSWERS PAGE 152

WE HAVE NO IDEA HOW THE BRAIN ARRIVES AT MOST OF THE DECISIONS IT MAKES, but current computers are very different. Computers can't do anything until we tell them *exactly* what to do, which we do by writing computer programs—known as coding.

Computer programs work by running a specific set of instructions in the order they are given, with the computer continuing to follow instructions until the program says that it's finished.

The set of blocks on the opposite page provide a visual version of a simple computer program. You could create this program on a computer and run it to see what it does, but instead you're going to run the program yourself—using your brain!

RUNNING THE PROGRAM

Begin at the START circle, then follow the arrows one at a time to do what the instructions tell you. You will need the following explanations of each step:

1. Create a variable called **counter** and set its current value to 1. Write this number in the orange box to keep track of its current value. A "variable" is a value stored by a computer. It's called a variable because it can ... vary!

2. Create a variable called **text,** and set its value to the eight letters **WDEOLNLE.** We won't change the value of this variable, so no need to make a copy of its current value.

3. Find the letter at position **counter** from the variable **text** and copy it to the first empty space in the green box. For example, if **counter** is 1, then you should take the first letter, *W,* and write it in the first spot in the green box. If **counter** is 3, you should take the third letter, and so on.

4. Find the letter at position **counter** +1 from the variable **text,** and copy it to the first empty space in the blue box. Because of the +1, if **counter** is equal to 1, then you should copy the **second** letter to the blue box, or if **counter** is 3, then you would copy the **fourth** letter.

5. Increase the value of **counter** by 2, so if it was 1 before, then you now change it to 3. Write its new value in the orange box, crossing out the old value.

6. If the value of **counter** is **less than** 8, go back to step 3 and continue following the arrows. Otherwise, you are finished.

RESULT

You will end up with a four-letter word in the green box and a four-letter word in the blue box. You should know if you are correct because you will have written a relevant two-word phrase!

CHANGING THE PROGRAM

If you understand how the program works, are you up to the challenge of making it write out something different?

Imagine that the green and blue boxes are now empty again. If you are allowed to change only **one** instruction box (1 to 6), then how would you make the program write out "BOOKENDS"?

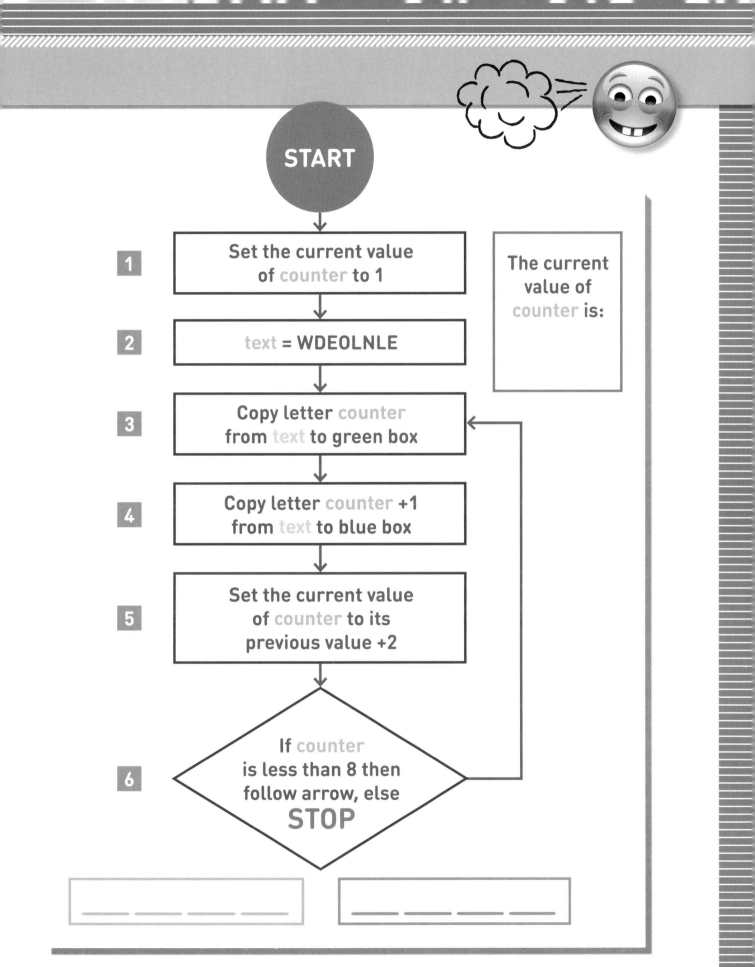

START

1 — Set the current value of counter to 1

2 — text = WDEOLNLE

3 — Copy letter counter from text to green box

4 — Copy letter counter +1 from text to blue box

5 — Set the current value of counter to its previous value +2

6 — If counter is less than 8 then follow arrow, else **STOP**

The current value of counter is:

_ _ _ _ _ _   _ _ _ _ _ _

TiME TRiALS

WORD FIT ANSWERS PAGE 152

Place all of the words into the grid, one letter per box, so that every word can be found reading either across or down within the puzzle.

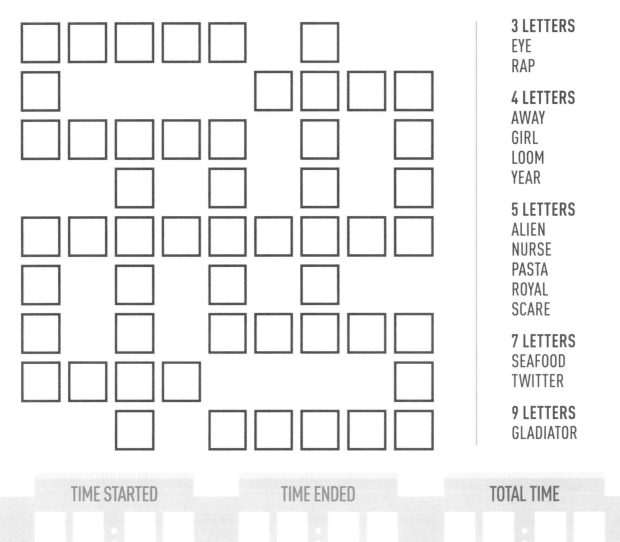

3 LETTERS
EYE
RAP

4 LETTERS
AWAY
GIRL
LOOM
YEAR

5 LETTERS
ALIEN
NURSE
PASTA
ROYAL
SCARE

7 LETTERS
SEAFOOD
TWITTER

9 LETTERS
GLADIATOR

TIME STARTED

TIME ENDED

TOTAL TIME

BUILDING FENCES ANSWERS PAGE 152

Join all of the dots to draw a line that travels through every dot continuously and makes one single loop. To get you started, some dots have already been joined. You can use only horizontal and vertical lines to join dots, and the loop can't cross over itself or use any dot more than once.

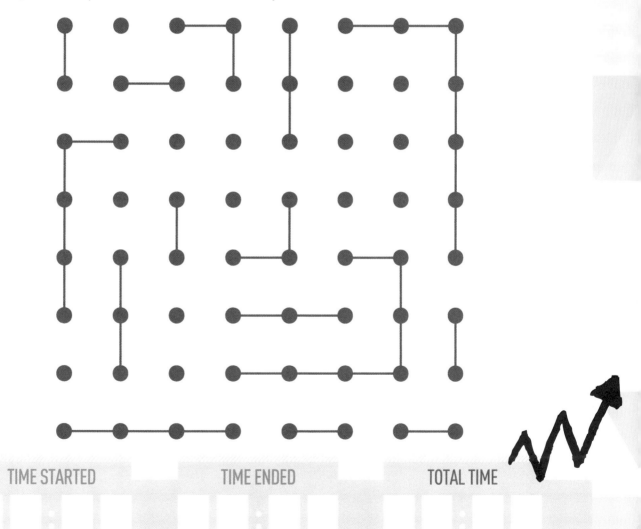

TIME STARTED

TIME ENDED

TOTAL TIME

CHAPTER **TWO**

MIRROR, MIRROR PAGE 28, TOP
The pictures are of a bottle, an anchor, a star, a diamond, and a padlock:

WORD FIT PAGE 32

MAYOR C
  I   POOR
CREAM N A
  M   O C F
IMPATIENT
R E O A
I R RULES
SMOG   U
  R CLIMB

BUILDING FENCES PAGE 33

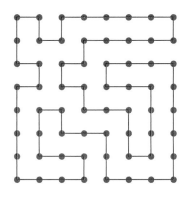

CHAPTER **THREE**

ROUNDABOUT WORD SEARCH
PAGE 35

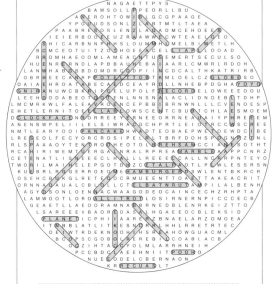

MULTI-ANAGRAMS PAGE 38
NWO: NOW, OWN, WON
TRA: ART, RAT, TAR
ETA: ATE, EAT, TEA (and also ETA itself is a word—it's a Greek letter—so there are actually four anagrams here!)
APSW: PAWS, SWAP, WASP
ANPS: NAPS, PANS, SNAP, SPAN
OPST: POST, POTS, SPOT, STOP, TOPS

THEMED ANAGRAM SETS PAGE 39, TOP
FRUITS: Peach, Orange, Plum, Mango, Lime, Strawberry, Grape, Pineapple, Tangerine; **ANIMALS:** Horse, Snail, Goat, Snake, Lion, Wolf, Owl, Bat, Hamster

WORD PYRAMID PAGE 39, BOTTOM
1) CAT, 2) FACT, 3) CRAFT, 4) FACTOR
5) FACTORY

WORD RIDDLES PAGE 40, TOP
• The letter *e*
• In a dictionary
• The word "misspelled," answering the literal question as to which of the words is the word "misspelled"—the word itself is spelled correctly.

CODE-CRACKING I PAGE 40, BOTTOM LEFT
The code is that the first and last letters of each word have been swapped, so for example WORD would be written as DROW. The phrases are: DON'T COUNT YOUR CHICKENS BEFORE THEY HATCH; ONCE IN A BLUE MOON; A BLESSING IN DISGUISE

CODE-CRACKING II PAGE 40, BOTTOM RIGHT
AT THE DROP OF A HAT; SIT ON THE FENCE; ACTIONS SPEAK LOUDER THAN WORDS

REVEAL THE PHRASE PAGE 41
One in a million ("1" inside 1,000,000, i.e. a million), Red tape, Bounce back ("Bounce" written backward), Over the moon (arrows pointing over "the moon"), Fall down ("FALL" written downward)

CLASSIC CROSSWORD PAGE 42

M	I	N	U	T	E		D	R	U	G
O		O		O		W		I		I
T	W	O		W	H	I	S	P	E	R
O		D		E		N				L
R	U	L	E	R		G	L	A	S	S
		E						I		
N	A	S	T	Y		S	T	R	A	W
O				O		O		P		A
V	A	N	I	L	L	A		O	W	L
E		A		K		R		R		
L	E	G	S		S	T	A	T	U	S

Bonus answer: WORD GAMES

ARROW WORD PAGE 43

	A		B		M		W	
	P	R	E	D	A	T	O	R
S	T	A	G		C		R	
		M		B	A	W	L	S
	F		S		R	I	D	E
H	O	R	I	Z	O	N		A
	E	E	L		N		C	
		V	E	H	I	C	L	E
A	R	E	N	A		L	A	Y
		A	C	T		U	S	E
M	A	L	E		M	E	S	S

A–Z CROSSWORD PAGE 44

SPIRAL CROSSWORD PAGE 45

Inward		Outward	
1-6	GARDEN	50-48	ROT
7-9	INK	47-45	AID
10-12	CAR	44-39	ARTIST
13-15	TOO	38-36	RAM
16-18	RAG	35-31	STAFF
19-23	NAKED	30-28	RAW
24-26	ACE	27-22	DECADE
27-31	DWARF	21-14	KANGAROO
32-34	FAT	13-9	TRACK
35-39	SMART	8-5	NINE
40-42	SIT	4-1	DRAG
43-50	RADIATOR		

WORD SEARCH MANIA PAGES 46–47

FLOWERS: ANEMONE, ASTER, BEGONIA, BUTTERCUP, CARNATION, DAFFODIL, FOXGLOVE, FUCHSIA, LAVENDER, MARIGOLD, ORCHID, PETUNIA, SNAPDRAGON, SNOWDROP, SUNFLOWER, TULIP

COLORS: BLACK, BLUE, BROWN, CRIMSON, CYAN, GRAY, GREEN, INDIGO, LILAC, MAGENTA, ORANGE, PINK, SAFFRON, SILVER, WHITE, YELLOW

NAMES: AMBER, ASH, AZALEA, DAISY, HAZEL, IRIS, JADE, LIAM, LILY, MASON, NOAH, OLIVE, POPPY, ROSE, RUBY, VIOLET

REVERSIBLE WORDS PAGE 48, TOP
Reward / Drawer, Trap / Part, Repaid / Diaper, Spoons / Snoops

PALINDROMIC WORDS PAGE 48, BOTTOM
Ewe, Pup, Noon, Level, Rotor, Solos

ZIGZAG PAGE 49

WORD SQUARE PAGE 50, LEFT
Words include ace, aced, act, acted, action, actioned, ate, atone, atoned, cat, cation, cud, cue, cued, den, doe, don, done, dot, dote, duct, due, duet, eat, end, eon, eta, ion, iota, neat, net, nod, node, not, note, noted, ode, one, tea, ten, tend, tie, tied, toe, toed, ton, tone, and toned. The bonus word using all the letters is "education."

WORD MASH-UP PAGE 50, RIGHT
• BLACK and WHITE
• APPLES and ORANGES
• CHUTES and LADDERS
• CUT and PASTE
• SKULL and CROSSBONES

WORD SLIDER PAGE 51, TOP
Words that you can find include SEALS, SEARS, SEEDS, SEERS, SHADE, SHALE, SHALL, SHARE, SHEDS, SHELL, SOARS, TEALS, TEARS, THERE, TOADS, WEALS, WEARS, WEEDS, WHALE, WHERE, and, of course, WORDS.

ANSWERS

HIDDEN WORDS PAGE 51, BOTTOM

Lion, Tiger, Bear, Mouse, Frog, Horse

STAR POWER WORD SEARCH PAGE 52

The entries, once the word "STAR" is converted to a star, look like this:

ALL-★	MOVIE ★
CO★ICA	NON★TER
CU★D	OUT★E
DA★DLY	RE★TED
DEATH ★	ROCK ★
DWARF ★	SHOOTING ★
FALSE ★T	★BOARD
GOLD ★	★CH
KICK ★T	★DOM
LONE ★ STATE	★LET
MEGA★	UP★T

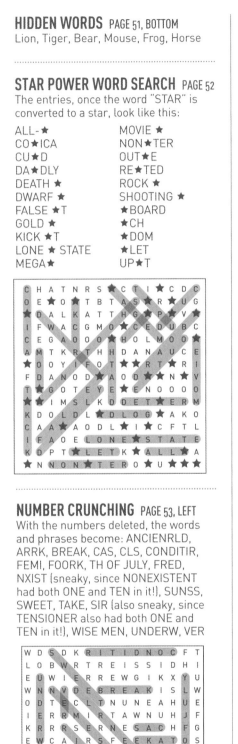

NUMBER CRUNCHING PAGE 53, LEFT

With the numbers deleted, the words and phrases become: ANCIENRLD, ARRK, BREAK, CAS, CLS, CONDITIR, FEMI, FOORK, TH OF JULY, FRED, NXIST (sneaky, since NONEXISTENT had both ONE and TEN in it!), SUNSS, SWEET, TAKE, SIR (also sneaky, since TENSIONER also had both ONE and TEN in it!), WISE MEN, UNDERW, VER

WORD NET PAGE 53, RIGHT

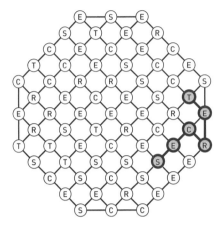

WORD FIT PAGE 54

BUILDING FENCES PAGE 55

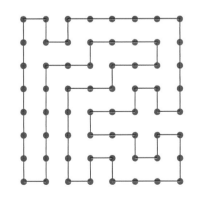

CHAPTER FOUR

REFLECTED CLOCKS PAGE 57

The times are as follows:

ROTATED SHAPES PAGE 60, TOP

1. C; 2. B

ROTATE THE IMAGE PAGE 60, BOTTOM

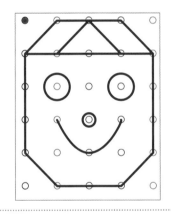

FIND THE MATCHING PAIR PAGE 61

A and F are identical.

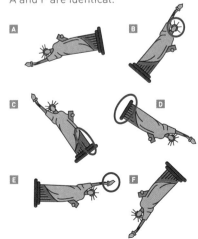

FOLDING IN HALF PAGE 62

1. D; 2. B

FOLDING AND PUNCHING PAGE 63

1. D; 2. B

SILHOUETTES PAGE 64

Silhouette D

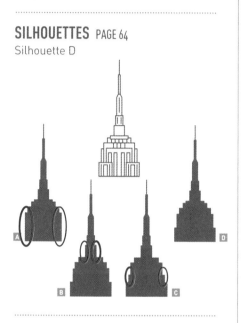

SPOT THE INVERSE PAGE 65, LEFT

Building C

INVERSE GRIDS PAGE 65, RIGHT

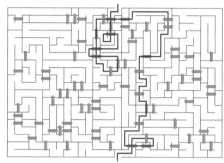

OVER AND UNDER MAP PAGE 66

Map One: C

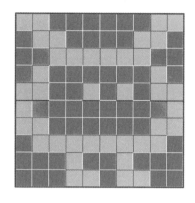

Map Two: D

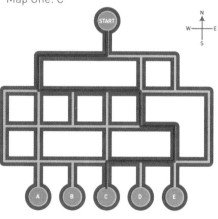

BRIDGE MAZE PAGE 67

COUNTING SHAPES PAGE 68

There are 29 rectangles and 18 triangles.

OVERLAPPING PICTURES PAGE 69

There are 10 dolphins: 8 of one size and 2 of a larger size. They are a little easier to count when the larger and smaller ones are given different colors:

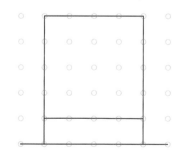

ODD CUBE OUT PAGE 70

1. D; 2. C; 3. A; 4. E

MATCHING CUBES PAGE 71

1. B; 2. B; 3. B; 4. D

DIRECT DIRECTIONS PAGE 72

ANSWERS

RELATIVE DIRECTIONS PAGE 73

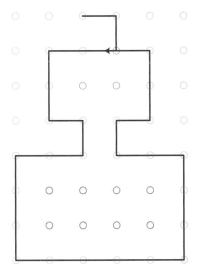

JIGSAW PIECES PAGE 74

G, D, B, F

NUMBER LINK PAGE 75, LEFT

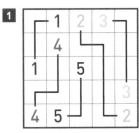

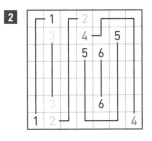

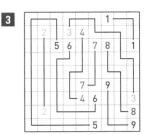

CIRCUIT BOARD PAGE 75, RIGHT

Piece 1

WORD FIT PAGE 76

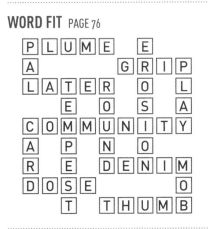

BUILDING FENCES PAGE 77

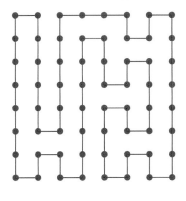

CHAPTER **FIVE**

ROTATIONAL PICTURE PAGE 79

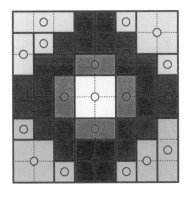

MATH MACHINES PAGE 82

Puzzle 1: 12, since 10 x 2 = 20; 20 + 20 = 40; 40 ÷ 5 = 8; 8 + 20 = 28; 28 ÷ 7 = 4; 4 × 3 = 12

Puzzle 2: 4, since 21 ÷ 3 = 7; 7 + 2 = 9; 9 × 2 = 18; 18 ÷ 3 = 6; 6 × 5 = 30; 30 + 14 = 44; 44 ÷ 11 = 4

MATH MATCHING PAGE 83, TOP

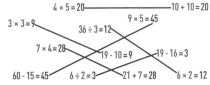

ROMAN NUMERAL MATH
PAGE 83, BOTTOM

II + III = V, since 2 + 3 = 5
VI + V = XI, since 6 + 5 = 11
X + LI = LXI, since 10 + 51 = 61
X + L + V + C = CLXV, since 10 + 50 + 5 + 100 = 165

DOMINO CHAIN PAGE 84

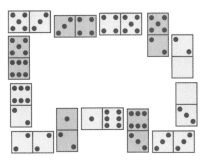

DOMINO PLACEMENT PAGE 85, LEFT

5			6		5	4	
5	2	3	3	3	1	1	6
1	6	4	4	3	2	1	1
5	6	3		4	1	5	4
2	2	5			4	5	4
3	6	2	1	6	6	2	2
6	4	2	5		1	3	3

DOMINO MATH PAGE 85, RIGHT

Red domino: The left-hand side could be a 3 or 5; the right-hand side could be a 4, 5, or 6.
Blue domino: The domino could be a 1:6, a 3:6, or a 5:6.

CARD PROBABILITY PAGE 86, LEFT

2 in 4, since there are 2 red suits out the total of 4 different suits. This can also be written as 1 in 2, by dividing both numbers by 2.
4 in 52, since there are 4 "7"s in the pack of 52 cards. This can also be written as 1 in 13, by dividing both numbers by 4.
12 in 51, since there are 12 cards of the same suit left of the 51 remaining in the pack after you have dealt the first card.

CARD LOGIC PAGE 86, RIGHT

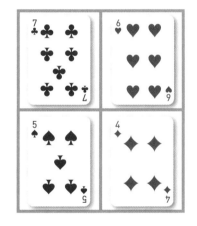

DICE SIDES PAGE 87, TOP

The total of the underneath sides is 3 + 4 + 2 + 1 + 4 + 1 + 6 = 21.

DICE MATH PAGE 87, BOTTOM

1 in 6
2 in 6 (since there are 2 possibilities); this can also be written as 1 in 3
4 in 6 (since there are 4 possibilities: 3, 4, 5, or 6); this can also be written as 2 in 3
1 in 6; whatever you roll first, you then have a 1 in 6 chance of rolling the same number on the second die roll

CIRCLE LINK PAGE 88

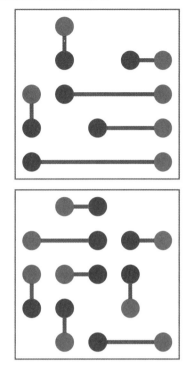

BRIDGES PAGE 89

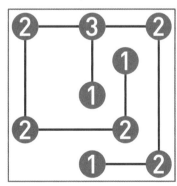

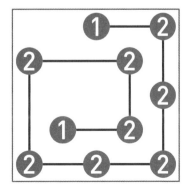

SUDOKU PAGE 90

4x4

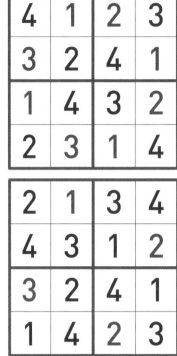

6x6

5	1	2	6	4	3
6	3	4	5	2	1
3	5	1	2	6	4
4	2	6	1	3	5
1	6	3	4	5	2
2	4	5	3	1	6

4	3	6	1	5	2
5	1	2	6	3	4
1	4	3	5	2	6
6	2	5	4	1	3
3	6	1	2	4	5
2	5	4	3	6	1

ANSWERS

ODD & EVEN SUDOKU PAGE 91, TOP

Place 1 to 4

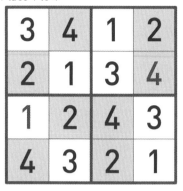

Place 1 to 6

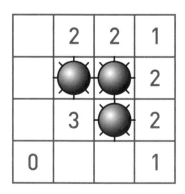

MINDSWEEPER PAGE 91, BOTTOM

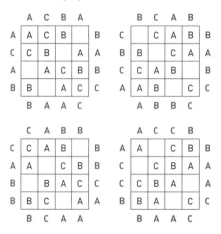

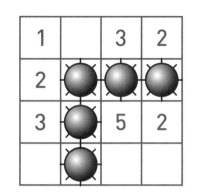

EASY AS A, B, C PAGE 92

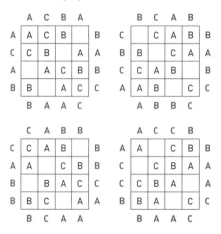

TOUCHY LETTERS PAGE 93

Touchy 5x5

B	E	C	A	D
A	D	B	E	C
E	C	A	D	B
D	B	E	C	A
C	A	D	B	E

C	A	D	B	E
D	B	E	C	A
E	C	A	D	B
A	D	B	E	C
B	E	C	A	D

Touchy 6x6

C	E	B	D	A	F
D	A	F	C	E	B
F	C	E	B	D	A
B	D	A	F	C	E
A	F	C	E	B	D
E	B	D	A	F	C

D	E	F	B	C	A
B	C	A	D	E	F
E	F	B	C	A	D
A	D	E	F	B	C
F	B	C	A	D	E
C	A	D	E	F	B

COLOR BY MATH PAGES 94–95

DOT-TO-DOT X3 PAGE 96

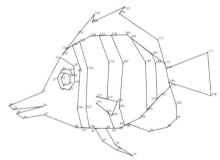

DON'T LIFT YOUR PEN PAGE 97

Did you figure it out? The picture on the left can't be traced without lifting your pen, whereas the one on the right can be. One possible solution is:

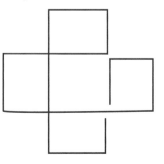

WORD FIT PAGE 98

BUILDING FENCES PAGE 99

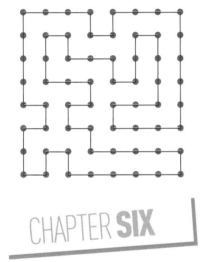

CHAPTER SIX

MATCHING PEOPLE PAGE 105
There are 10 matching faces.

GRID RECALL PAGE 108
The resulting picture is a close-up of a smiley face:

DOT CONNECTIONS PAGE 109

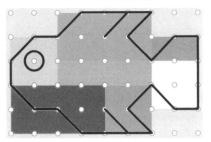

SUBSTITUTIONS PAGE 112
Circled items: vacuum, plate, gold lamp, remote control
Missing objects: blue clip, TV, scissors, silver lamp

ADDITIONS PAGE 113
Extra pieces added:

What's missing from the left side: one blueberry, one pineapple, two strawberries, one raspberry

COLOR RECALL PAGE 114

DOTTY TEST PAGE 115

MEMORY MATH PAGE 117
16; 8; 2 and 9; 19

WORD FIT PAGE 120

ANSWERS

BUILDING FENCES PAGE 121

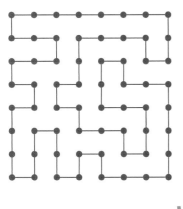

CHAPTER **SEVEN**

IT MUST BE OBVIOUS PAGE 123

SPOT THE COLOR-BY-PIXEL DIFFERENCE PAGES 126–127

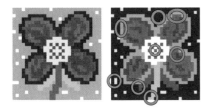

WORD HUNT PAGES 128–129

1) **Possible words include:**
   4 letters: blue, buff, cyan, gold, gray, jade, lime, navy, pink, rose, ruby, rust, sand, teal
   6 letters: bronze, cherry, copper, indigo, maroon, orange, purple, salmon, silver, violet, yellow
2) **Possible words include:**
   5 letters: apple, grape, lemon, mango, melon, peach
   6 letters: banana, cherry, orange, papaya, tomato, lychee
   9 letters: blueberry, cranberry, kiwifruit, nectarine, pineapple, raspberry, tangerine
3) **Possible words include:**
   3 letters: red
   5 letters: green
4) **Possible words include:**
   4 letters: pear, plum
   6 letters: orange
   10 letters: strawberry
5) **Possible words include:**
   3 letters: tan
   5 letters: beige, mauve, white
6) **Possible words include:**
   4 letters: lime
   6 letters: banana
   10 letters: watermelon

ARTIFICIAL BRAINS PAGES 140–141

The original program writes "WELL" in the green box and "DONE" in the blue box to make the phrase "WELL DONE."

To write out "BOOKENDS" you should change step 2 so that it reads as follows: text = BEONODKS

WORD FIT PAGE 142

BUILDING FENCES PAGE 143

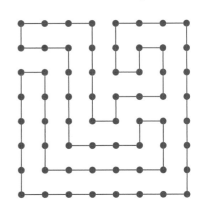

MAKE YOUR OWN WORD SEARCH!

HAVE YOU EVER WONDERED HOW PUZZLES ARE WRITTEN OR WANTED TO WRITE YOUR OWN TO ENTERTAIN YOUR FAMILY AND FRIENDS? THIS BOOK IS PACKED FULL OF LOTS OF DIFFERENT TYPES OF PUZZLES, BUT HERE'S THE INSIDE SCOOP ON HOW TO MAKE ONE OF THE MOST POPULAR PUZZLE TYPES: WORD SEARCHES.

CHOOSING YOUR WORDS

Creating word searches is a lot of fun. You can put any words you want in them, but they're even more fun when they are themed around a topic. This makes a puzzle more interesting to solve, because you can often spot words in the grid even before you find them on the clue list. And if you make your own puzzle, you can choose a set of words based around your family, your friends, or your school, making a puzzle that's really personal to you.

When you are writing your list of words, try to avoid words that include all the letters of another word on your list. So, for example, it's best not to hide SUPERMAN and MAN in the same grid, because then there would be a MAN hidden completely within SUPERMAN, so it would be confusing when you tried solving the word search. (You might think you'd found MAN, when in fact you'd found SUPERMAN.) Because words can be written backward in word searches, you should check your word list for words that can be found in reverse inside other words, too. For example, if you had FLOWER on your list, then it would be best not to also include WOLF, because when solving the puzzle you might accidentally find the WOLF that's hidden backward at the start of FLOWER.

CREATING THE GRID

Once you have a list of words you'd like to hide in the grid, you can look at the words and decide how big a grid to create. Whatever the longest word is, you'll need a grid that's at least that wide or that tall. So if your longest word is 12 letters long, your grid will need to be 12 or more rows or columns wide. You might want to make it a bit bigger than you need for the longest word, however, so you have space to fit in lots more words, too.

Draw out an empty grid, or use square graph paper

SUPER DOG!

TURN THE PAGE TO MAKE YOUR OWN WORD SEARCH AND STUMP YOUR FRIENDS!

if you have it handy. Start by writing your longest word in the grid, with one letter per grid square. (It's fun to put it at a diagonal, so it's harder to spot!) Cross it out on your list of words you want to fit, so you remember that you've already written it in. Then, after you've done that, find the next longest word and see if you can fit it into the grid in such a way that it shares a letter with the word you have already added. So if the first word was "ELEPHANT" and your next word is "CAMEL," it would be great to overlap one of the *E*'s of ELEPHANT with the *E* of CAMEL. If you can't overlap the words, you can try looking down your word list for one that can overlap. Word searches are more fun when the words cross over one another— although they don't have to. It will still be an awesome word search puzzle even if they don't.

ADDING THE FINISHING TOUCHES

Finally, to finish off your puzzle you need to write a letter in all the empty spaces. This could be any letter in each space, from A to Z. But if you want to make your puzzle even more tricky, stick to the letters that you have used in the hidden words. For example, if none of your words have an *X* in them, then don't write an *X* in any of the leftover spaces. It's also important to try not to form any accidental new words while writing the letters in, so make sure you don't form a second copy of any of the words on your word list. Also try to be careful not to accidentally form other words that you don't want to be found.

Now you can write out a list of all the words you've used in the puzzle, and it's ready for people to solve! It's nice to sort the word list into alphabetical order, so it's easy to check for words in it, but this isn't essential. You can have them in any order you want.

IDEAS FOR OTHER AWESOME WORD SEARCHES

Once you've made your first word search, you might want to make some more. Apart from choosing different topics and sizes, one way to make a really personal word search is to create a grid that is an unusual shape. For example, you could lay out the squares in the shape of a flower when making a seasonal puzzle or in a circle if you are hiding the names of shapes—a bit like the puzzle on page 35 of this book (although you don't need as many words and letters as that particular puzzle!).

Another way you could make an unusual word search would be to not give people the word list. You could instead just give them the topic and perhaps the first letter of each word (and also its length in letters, if you are feeling generous!). Then people would have to just search through the grid to find the hidden words.

As you become a word search expert, you can also come up with your own ideas for special word search puzzles. You could write the words into the grid in L shapes instead of straight lines, for example, or if you were really trying to make it tricky you could try jumbling the letters of the word when writing them into the grid (but that would be really hard to solve). That's OK, though: The fun thing about making your own puzzle is that you can use whatever rules you want!

CREATE YOUR OWN PUZZLE

▶▶▶ NAME YOUR WORD SEARCH: _____

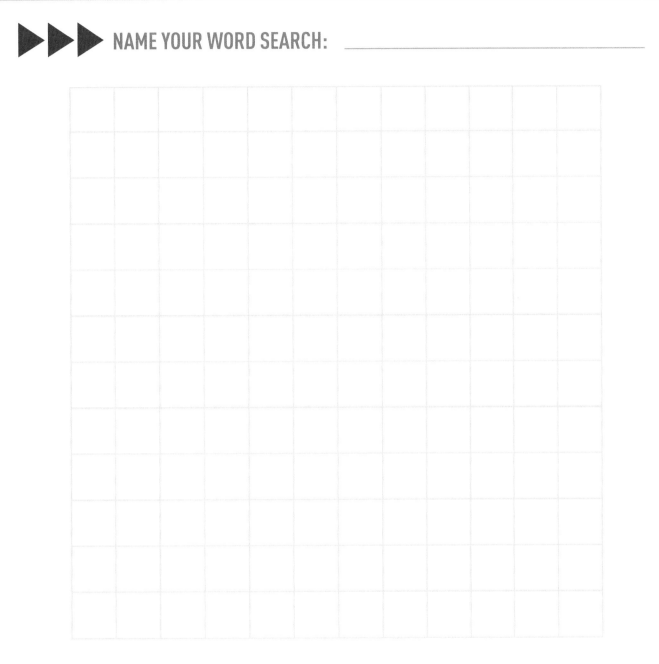

WORD BANK

INDEX

Boldface indicates illustrations.

INDEX

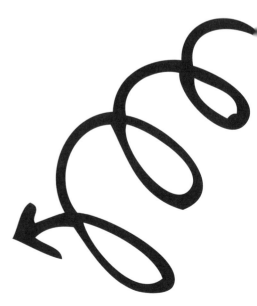

PHOTO CREDITS

ALL PUZZLE ART BY DR. GARETH MOORE UNLESS NOTED BELOW.

SS=SHUTTERSTOCK
COVER: (BACKGROUND), GRANDEDUC/SS; (GLOBE), TITOVSTUDIO/DREAMSTIME; (DOODLES), PAKET/SS; (ARROW), JOHAVEL/SS; (BIRD), PRAPASS/SS; (PINWHEEL), CHRISTOPHER ELWELL/DREAMSTIME; (ELEPHANT), NAMAKUKI/SS; (SELFIE), NICOLASMENIJES/DREAMSTIME; (TOY), GRANTOTUFO/DREAMSTIME; (AIRPLANE), PHOTODISC; **SPINE:** PAKET/SS; **BACK COVER:** (EMOJI), OBER-ART/SS; (ARROW), JOHAVEL/SS; (SHEEP), N-SKY/SS; (FLOWERS), PAKET/SS

FRONT MATTER: 2-3 (BRAIN BACKGROUND THROUGHOUT), GRANDEDUC/SS; 2 (UP), CHONES/SS; 2 (LO), HANNAMARIAH/SS; 3 (CTR RT) PRAPASS/SS; 4 (DOODLES THROUGHOUT), PAKET/SS; 4 (LO), INXTI/SS; 5 (UP), MEGO STUDIO/SS; 5 (LO LE), TANG YAN SONG/SS; 5 (LO RT), TITOVSTUDIO/DREAMSTIME; **CHAPTER ONE:** 6 (STICKY PAPER THROUGHOUT), MARTINA VACULIKOVA/SS; 6 (UP), PIO3/SS; 6 (LO LE), MAGDALENA SKRZYPCZAK/SS; 8-9 (HEXAGON BACKGROUND THROUGHOUT), YANIE/SS; 8 (DOODLES), PIO3/SS; 8 (LO), SSPL/GETTY IMAGES; 9 (UP LE), UNIVERSAL HISTORY ARCHIVE/UIG VIA GETTY IMAGES; 9 (UP RT), WELLCOME IMAGES/SCIENCE SOURCE; 9 (CTR RT), SS / EVERETT HISTORICAL; 11 (BRAIN), JEONG SUH/BRYAN CHRISTIE DESIGN; 11 (LO), MINDSCAPE STUDIO/SS; **CHAPTER TWO:** 14 (LO), DENVER POST/GETTY IMAGES; 15 (UP LE), BETH RUGGIERO-YORK/SS; 15 (UP RT), Y PHOTO STUDIO/SS; (CTR LE), ODUA IMAGES/SS; 15 (CTR RT), SERGEY URYAD-NIKOV/SS; 15 (LO), ART KONOVALOV/SS; 17 (ARROWS THROUGHOUT), JOHAVEL/SS; 17 (LO), AFRICA STUDIO/SS; 18 (EMOJIS THROUGHOUT), OBER-ART/SS; 23 (UP RT), OLGA POPOVA/SS; 23 (LO LE), AFRICA STUDIO/SS; 24-25 (BACKGROUND), ANNA/SS; 26-27 (BACKGROUND), TORSAK THAMMACHOTE/SS; 28 (UP), PHOTOMONTAGE/SS; 29 (LO), NINAMALYNA/SS; 30-31 (BACKGROUND), PATRYK KOSMIDER/SS; 30 (UP), WAVEBREAKMEDIA/SS; 30 (LO), KAYO/SS; 32-33 (TRIANGLES THROUGHOUT), GRANDEDUC/SS; **CHAPTER THREE:** 37 (UP LE), CHAJAMP/SS; 37 (UP RT), BARTOSZ HADYNIAK/GETTY IMAGES; 37 (CTR), INSIGHTS/UIG/BRIDGEMAN IMAGES; 37 (LIGHTBULB), PIETRO/SS; 37 (LO), ROMAN023_PHOTOGRAPHY/SS; 38 (UP), SUPERHEANG168/SS; 38 (LO), FLYDRAGON/SS; 41 (UP), PROSTOCK-STUDIO/SS; 41 (LO), CLAUDIO DIVIZIA/SS; 42 (UP), RVLSOFT/SS; 45, INK DROP/SS; 46-47 (BACKGROUND), AKUGASAHAGY/SS; 46 (UP), QUANG HO/SS; 47 (UP LE), DAVE BREDESON/DREAMSTIME; 47 (UP CTR), QUANG HO/SS; 47 (UP RT), KUCHER SERHII/SS; 47 (LO), QUANG HO/SS; 48 (LO), IVANOVA N/SS; 49 (UP), NIRADJ/SS; 49 (LO), N-SKY/SS; 50 (UP), MAREKULIASZ/SS; 51 (LO), NESRUDHEEN MATATHOOR/SS; 52-53 (BACKGROUND), AOPSAN/SS; 53 (UP), FEDBUL/SS; 55 (UP), LEV KROPOTOV/SS; **CHAPTER FOUR:** 57 (CLOCKS), RTIMAGES/SS; 58 (LO), ERASHOV/SS; 59 (UP LE), DUKAI PHOTOGRAPHER/GETTY IMAGES; 59 (UP RT), MONKEY BUSINESS IMAGES/SS; 59 (CTR RT), FEDOROV OLEKSIY/SS; 59 (LIGHTBULB), PIETRO/SS; 59 (PHONE), VADIM GEORGIEV/SS; 59 (LO RT), ADRAGAN/SS; 61 (RT), DIBROVA/SS; 62 (UP), STUART MILES/SS; 63 (UP RT), OKSANA SHUFRYCH/SS; 64-65 (LO), DIBROVA/SS; 67 (LO), CIGDEM/SS; 68-69, DARIOS/SS; 72 (PENS), RIMMAORPHEY/SS; 74, LUNJA/SS; 74 (A), BILDAGENTUR ZOONAR GMBH/SS; 77 (UP), LEV KROPOTOV/SS; **CHAPTER FIVE:** 79 (LO RT), SOFIAWORLD/SS; 80 (UP), BOGUSLAWA KOZIARSKA/SS; 80 (LO LE), FLASHON STUDIO/SS; 81 (UP LE), MONKEY BUSINESS IMAGES/SS; 81 (UP RT), COZINE/SS; 81 (CTR), GUILLERMO PIS GONZALEZ/SS; 83 (LO), INXTI/SS; 84 (UP), DR TRAVEL PHOTO AND VIDEO/SS; 86 (CTR), PANDAWILD/SS; 86 (LO), ADMIN/SS; 87 (LO), TANG YAN SONG/SS; 88 (UP), FIVESPOTS/SS; 89 (LO), EBTIKAR/SS; 92-93 (BACKGROUND), TATIANA53/SS; 94 (SPLATS), ADMIN/SS; 96-97 (FISH), MIRKO ROSENAU/SS; 96 (LO RT), VALIZA/SS; 97 (UP RT), JANTANA/SS; 99 (UP), LEV KROPO-TOV/SS; **CHAPTER SIX:** 100 (UMBRELLA), VENIAMIN KRASKOV/SS; 100 (BALL), KOOSEN/SS; 100 (CANOE), SMILEUS/SS; 102, TEREKHOV IGOR/SS; 103 (UP), HERBERT KRATKY/SS; 103 (CTR LE), RAWF8/SS; 103 (CTR RT), DARREN BAKER/SS; 103 (LIGHTBULB), PIETRO/SS; 104 (AIDEN), ZURIJETA/SS; 104 (MING), LEUNGCHOPAN/SS; 104 (EMMA), EVGENIIA TRUSHKOVA/SS; 104 (LIAM), DJOMAS/SS; 104 (OLIVIA), COOKIE STUDIO/SS; 104 (LUCAS), DAXIAO PRODUCTIONS/SS; 104 (SAMIRA), SZEFEI/SS; 104 (ASHA), SAMUEL BORGES PHOTOGRAPHY/SS; 105 (ROW 1 (LEFT TO RIGHT): (1), DR-IMAGES/SS; (2), HANS KIM/SS; (3), SAMUEL BORGES PHOTOGRAPHY/SS; (4), DMYTRO VIETROV/SS; (5), ANDY DEAN PHOTOGRAPHY/SS; (6), DJOMAS/SS; (7), DAXIAO PRODUCTIONS/SS; (8), SEMENTSOVA LESIA/SS; (9), SZEFEI/SS; (10), SLP_LON-DON/SS; ROW 2 (LEFT TO RIGHT): (1), HANS KIM/SS; (2), DAXIAO PRODUCTIONS/SS; (3), SLP_LONDON/SS; (4), EUROBANKS/SS; (5), LUIS SANTOS/SS; (6), DAXIAO PRO-DUCTIONS/SS; (7), COOKIE STUDIO/SS; (8), WAYHOME STUDIO/SS; (9), MAKISTOCK/SS; (10), MAKISTOCK/SS; ROW 3 (LEFT TO RIGHT): (1), PATHDOC/SS; (2), HANS KIM/SS; (3), TOM WANG/SS; (4), WAYHOME STUDIO/SS; (5), PATHDOC/SS; (6), ASHTPRODUCTIONS/SS; (7), SLP_LONDON/SS; (8), SLP_LONDON/SS; (9), MAKISTOCK/SS; (10), WAYHOME STUDIO/SS; ROW 4 (LEFT TO RIGHT): (1), DJOMAS/SS; (2), COOKIE STUDIO/SS; (3), WAYHOME STUDIO/SS; (4), SZEFEI/SS; (5), PATHDOC/SS; (6), WAYHOME STUDIO/SS; (7), DAXIAO PRODUCTIONS/SS; (8), WAYHOME STUDIO/SS; (9), ANDY DEAN PHOTOGRAPHY/SS; 105 (PINS), RALF GEITHE/SS; 106-107 (BACKGROUND), ALEXANDER LUKATSKIY/SS; 108 (LO), HANNAMARIAH/SS; 111 (UP RT), IMAGES.ETC/SS; 111 (CTR LE), P MAXWELL PHOTOGRAPHY/SS; 111 (CTR RT), HAYATI KAYHAN/SS; 111 (LO), ON_FRANCE/SS; 111 (POOL), KROPIC1/SS; 112 (CLOTHESPIN), MICHAEL RANSBURG/SS; 112 (FLASHLIGHT), MOISES FER-NANDEZ ACOSTA/SS; 112 (TEAPOT), ALEKSEYKOLOTVIN/SS; 112 (HAIR DRYER), GORAN BOGICEVIC/SS; 112 (SPOON), BERND SCHMIDT/SS; 112 (SCISSORS), ARMIN STAUDT/SS; 112 (CABLE), SERGEY LE/SS; 112 (LAMP), JANNIWET/SS; 112 (PHONE), BOONTHIDA SRIJAK/SS; 112 (TV), RUSLAN IVANTSOV/SS; 112 (MIXER), M. UNAL OZMEN/SS; 112 (SILVERWARE), ONAIR/SS; 112 (PLATE), ANDREY_KUZMIN/SS; 112 (REMOTE), J. HELGASON/SS; 113 (BANANA), MAKS NARODENKO/SS; 113 (APPLE), TIM UR/SS; 113 (KIWI), MAX LASHCHEUSKI/SS; 113 (ORANGE), MAKS NARODENKO/SS; 113 (CHERRY), TIM UR/SS; 113 (PEAR), BERGAMONT/SS; 113 (COCONUT), IURII KACHKOVSKYI/SS; 113 (PINEAPPLE), JIRI MIKLO/SS; 113 (PEACH), DAVYDENKO YULIIA/SS; 113 (DRAGON FRUIT), ANASTASIIA SKOROBOGATOVA/SS; 113 (GRAPES), EVGENY KARANDAEV/SS; 113 (BLUEBERRY), TIM UR/SS; 113 (STRAWBERRY), MAKS NARODENKO/SS; 113 (RASPBERRY), ANNA KUCHEROVA/SS; 115, KIKOSTOCK/SS; 116-117 (BACKGROUND), PICSFIVE/SS; 116 (LE), ZEYNEP DEMIR/SS; 117 (UP), TALVI/SS; 118 (LE), MNSTUDIO/SS; 119 (UP), IASHA/SS; 119 (LO), PARANAMIR/SS; 121 (FENCE), BAERBEL SCHMIDT/GETTY IMAGES; **CHAPTER SEVEN:** 123 (SCHOOL), LEV KROPOTOV/SS; 123 (DINOS), FRANCO TEMPESTA; 124 (BALL), IASHA/SS; 125 (UP LE), SYDA PRODUCTIONS/SS; 125 (UP RT), DANNY E. HOOKS/SS; 125 (CTR RT), VCHAL/SS; 125 (LIGHTBULB), PIETRO/SS; 125 (LO LE), PHONLAMAI PHOTO/SS; 126 (LO), NADIIA KOROLSS; 128-129 (BACKGROUND), FUORIT3MPO/SS; 128 (UP), APPLE/SS; 130 (UP), JOVITTA/SS; 131 (UP), BLUEHAND/SS; 131 (LO LE), OLEKSANDR LYTVYNENKO/SS; 131 (LO RT), PHOTOVOVA/SS; 133 (CTR RT), SAMUEL BORGES PHOTOGRAPHY/SS; 134 (CTR), COOKIE STUDIO/SS; 134 (LO), MIZKIT/SS; 135, ANDREY KORSHENKOV/SS; 138-139 (BACKGROUND), KZWW/SS; 138, PROSTOCK-STUDIO/SS; 139 (UP), LAPINA/SS; 139 (CTR), PROSTOCK-STUDIO/SS; 139 (LO), MATT B/SS; 140 (LO), AFRICA STUDIO/SS; 143 (FENCE), LEV KROPOTOV/SS; **BACK MATTER:** 153, ALEXANDER MAZURKEVICH/SS

CREDITS

For all the nerds, geeks, and brainiacs —S.W.D.
For my wonderful family —G.M.

Since 1888, the National Geographic Society has funded more than 12,000 research, exploration, and preservation projects around the world. The Society receives funds from National Geographic Partners, LLC, funded in part by your purchase. A portion of the proceeds from this book supports this vital work. To learn more, visit natgeo.com/info.

For more information, visit nationalgeographic.com, call 1-800-647-5463, or write to the following address:

National Geographic Partners
1145 17th Street N.W.
Washington, D.C. 20036-4688 U.S.A.

Visit us online at nationalgeographic.com/books

For librarians and teachers: ngchildrensbooks.org

More for kids from National Geographic: natgeokids.com

National Geographic Kids magazine inspires children to explore their world with fun yet educational articles on animals, science, nature, and more. Using fresh storytelling and amazing photography, *Nat Geo Kids* shows kids ages 6 to 14 the fascinating truth about the world—and why they should care.
kids.nationalgeographic.com/subscribe

For information about special discounts for bulk purchases, please contact National Geographic Books Special Sales: specialsales@natgeo.com

For rights or permissions inquiries, please contact National Geographic Books Subsidiary Rights: bookrights@natgeo.com

Designed by Rachael Hamm Plett, Moduza Design

Trade paperback ISBN: 978-1-4263-3285-2

The publisher would like to acknowledge the following people for making this book possible: Stephanie Warren Drimmer, narrative text author; Dr. Gareth Moore, puzzle creator and puzzle text author; Jen Agresta, project editor; Michaela Weglinski, assistant editor; Brett Challos, art director; Sarah J. Mock, senior photo editor; Uliana Bazar and Matt Propert, photo editors; Alix Inchausti, production editor; Anne LeongSon and Gus Tello, design production assistants.

Printed in China
19/RRDS/1